A Conscious Life

NAVIGATING CRITICAL STAGES AND ASPECTS
OF LIFE SUCCESSFULLY

Funmi Oyetunji

Funmi Oyetunji
602, Munkenbeck
5 Hermitage Street
London, W2 1PW

Book Layout ©2017 BookDesignTemplates.com

Ordering Information:
Quantity sales. Special discounts are available on quantity purchases by corporations, associations, and others. For details, contact the "Special Sales Department" at the address above.

A Conscious Life / Funmi Oyetunji — 2nd ed.
Paperback ISBN 978-1-7391498-0-2
Hardback ISBN 978-1-7391498-1-9
E-Book ISBN 978-1-7391498-2-6

Contents

To my husband, Femi, and our lovely sons Abioye and Tosin, who have supported me as life unfolds.

For my descendants, praying them mindful and fulfilling lives.

In gratitude to my life's teachers, especially my grandmothers and my dad, who talked and still talk to me about all things pertaining to life.

Endorsements

A *Conscious Life* is a guide for successfully navigating critical stages and aspects of life.

A good man leaveth an inheritance to his children's children... I believe that the words in this book that Funmi Oyetunji has penned down are a priceless inheritance that her children to the nth generation will greatly benefit from.

A Life well lived is a gift from GOD. Funmi has been greatly blessed, and it is heartwarming that she now wants to be a blessing to many whom she will never know that will read her book.

Funmi pours out her life experiences in the book, beginning with the importance of a vision for life, being deliberate about life choices, and living a life of purpose. It then goes on to describe the different stages of life from childhood to young adulthood. A Conscious Life covers all the main aspects of life from education and learning to work and career, to the importance of financial literacy and how to attain financial freedom. [She covers] the importance of healthy relationships, marriage and parenting, coping with trauma and success, and health and spirituality and rounds up with how to age with grace and confidence.

I greatly recommend this book to all who seek wisdom and guidance in making key decisions. A Conscious Life summarizes in a simple and easy-to-read manner decades of experience, with practical examples that will help the reader successfully navigate life's journey.

Thank you, Funmi, for this enduring legacy.

—Sola David-Borha, Group CEO, Stanbic IBTC Bank, Nigeria

———

'A life lived without purpose is a wasted life.'

—Myles Munroe

A Conscious Life is the most detailed book I have yet read on the subject of living life, in which the author gives the reader a head's up in making the right choices through the business of life. She has taken the time, drawing on her own personal experiences and uncommon sense to help the reader through the important decisions everyone will make at the major intersections in life, choices of education, career, financial planning, marriage, parenting, health and fitness, etc.

Although I have thoroughly enjoyed reading the manuscript, I must say that it is not the kind of book you read and then forget; it will become a reference book which I am sure you will keep on referring to as you face tough choices. A must read, enjoy.

—Wale Adefarasin, General Overseer, Guiding Light Assembly, Nigeria

Foreword

The question is, "From where and when and how are we supposed to learn the art of living?"

Following deep reflections on her own life and the successes and failures of those around her, and the omissions and commissions that affected the respective outcomes, the author posed this rhetorical question in the preface to the book and thereafter proceeded to proffer answers to them in thirteen masterful chapters of flowing and readable prose illustrated with real-life experiences.

She proposes the adoption of a conscious life, where the owner leads a focussed life, takes charge and responsibility for the achievements and failures of his or her life by seeking and practising those values that conduce to a fulfilling existence.

The book benefits not only from the author's wide exposure but also from her familiarity with researches by experts and authorities on the various topics she explores, and the pages are spiced with quotations from those authorities and other anonymous persons.

The first four chapters deal mainly with issues concerning the young, from childhood to mature adulthood. Building self-confidence and adopting positive values are the foundation for success but are by no means the only key, and the ramifications are extensively explored in the book. Of special significance is building a vision and working towards it, pausing periodically to assess progress and making adjustments when necessary. Where the author speaks directly to the young adult, the language is neither pontifical nor magisterial but largely pedagogical.

The chapter on financial planning and wealth creation is a gem, and every individual who has an income ought to avail himself or herself of such counselling. The author's professional background, work, as well as her personal experience as a very successful investor has been deployed into producing this chapter which deserves to be a booklet on its own. It ends with an interesting discussion on estate (inheritance) planning and "the purpose and use of wealth".

Two other major chapters in the book are those on marriage and parenting, and they are the other main reasons why I expect the book to be intensely popular, especially among women and perceptive husbands.

Chapter 6, on family relationships and friendships, is mainly directed toward the young, although much of it applies to everyone. Of particular fascination is where the author recommends "different mates for different times and purposes". This utilitarian and liberalistic approach to friendship is widespread amongst older adults but much less appreciated amongst the young; for them, a friend is expected to be a friend for all seasons and purposes, which often leads to disappointments.

On marriage, the author discusses the various reasons that have been adduced for matrimony and its benefits to both husband and wife, also which ingredients to look for in selecting a spouse. More than half of that chapter –some eighteen pages – is devoted to the in-marriage experience, including interpersonal role expectations, the powerful role of money, and the gloomy subject of separation and divorce. Most spouses will find the author's positions to be realistic and practical.

The chapter on parenting was well illustrated with personal examples of the author, and any parent whose children have matured and left home will enjoy this chapter with knowing smiles. Younger parents will find useful principles to reflect upon and possibly adopt when an adolescent child appears to exhibit undue independence.

Chapter 9, on coping with and surmounting traumatic events, will no doubt be for many an adult reader the highlight of the book, particularly anyone who has either had the personal experience or observed a person who, having arduously attained an apogee of success and relative happiness, is suddenly beset with life's vicissitudes by which the person is dragged down into the trenches but through determination, assiduity, planning, and perhaps a helping hand or two, overcomes the travails and returns to life ascendant.

We are presented with the stories of four heroines: the author, who did not describe herself as one; her mother's marital crisis at the age of 18; and her two female friends: Pamela in London and Tola in Lagos. All through the chapter the prose is tender, sometimes sad, but always refreshing.

In the following chapter, the author attempts to define what constitutes a successful life and more broadly examines various facets thereof, including the management of success. Probably concerned that success almost always "gets into the head" of the subject, or perhaps because of her own observations of different types of successful people, the language changes to that of the preacher from the pulpit.

The rest of the book deals with the health of the human frame (exercise, appropriate nutrition and weight control, personal hygiene and proper grooming) and of the mind (worry, depression, and anger management), graceful ageing, and the subject of spirituality.

I congratulate Funmi Oyetunji for coming out with this laudable work. It recommends itself to adolescents and men and women of every age; it is a memorandum to the young adult who is desirous of a meaningful life, a handbook to brides and bridegrooms, a handmaiden for every parent, a manual on personal financial planning, and a fitting memorial to her grandmothers for their invaluable roles in shaping her own values during her formative years.

—Chief Ajibola Ogunshola, foremost actuary and Turnaround Chairman of The Punch (most widely read newspaper in Nigeria)

Preface

The subject of living interests me! I cannot help observing lives around me and wondering sometimes, "What happened there?" How did that life get to the point of my observation? I imagine what that person might have done to contribute to the success or failure of his or her own life. Usually, a life attracts my attention because of its exceptionality, whether good or bad. Over time, my observation turned to concern, especially as I came to see that many people seem to wander through life to just wake up one day, usually about middle age, and realise their lives happened while they weren't looking!

My concern grew as I noticed that even for the success stories, only a rare few had resulted from a conscious effort or vision of the person or those who had a critical influence on their lives. (By the way, when I adjudge a life successful, good, or accomplished, I am careful not to predicate my judgment on one index only, say just wealth or career success or only emotional stability. No, I am usually careful to look out for any lopsidedness that would signify imbalance. I believe only a life that has achieved a form of balance in most aspects can be adjudged to be truly successful, a life in which the person has obviously defined his or her own balance and can be seen to be sufficiently fulfilled therein.)

The question is, from where, and when and how are we supposed to learn the art of living? The school curriculum covers everything but the art (or the science) of living life. Apart from the lucky ones amongst us who get put through some form of cultural finishing school where life is looked at on a wider scale than just academics, or the very few that have been lucky to have been exposed to very active influences that have positively impacted them, the rest of us are schooled and scored from a very early age on the basis of academics only. It's as if once you're bright and getting good grades ... who needs life skills! Also, education is generally geared towards being able to get a livelihood at some stage. Whether that livelihood is in fact fulfilling is ofttimes ignored; meanwhile, all other matters that contribute to a full and joyful life are expected to happen without much consideration or help. But we know that nothing worthwhile happens without an uphill endeavour.

Unfortunately, traditional learning at home, which was the bedrock of cultural education, is also evaporating fast. The advent of both parents engaged in high profile and ultra-rewarding careers, leaving them too tired to teach their children, is not helping the situation. What was referred to as raising children is increasingly outsourced to play groups, nannies, and school.

The gap left by modernisation and the breakaway of nuclear family units from the traditional extended family was made clear to me after spending an afternoon in an airline lounge with a stranger as we waited for a delayed flight. An accomplished professional African female, Alice lamented what she called a tragic gap in the life of most educated Africans typified by her own story. She had moved from her East African culture in her teens to be educated in China where she dated and married a West African man. The failure of that relationship due to irreconcilable differences, when she tried to settle back with him in his home country, she believes could have been avoided if she'd had guidance before marriage. She attributed her naïveté in handling that important stage of choosing a life partner to not having had the cultural and life-skill advice usually received from the grandmother and many layers of relatives. According to her, what has been so lost has unfortunately not been replaced with any alternatives in the modern setting she was thrust into. She believes that gap often results in tragic consequences.

The Jewish community have a kind of 'finishing school' central to their mitzvah ceremonies (bar at 13 for the boy and bat at 12 for the girl) – a good age, I would say, to begin to have some clear ideas of what life is about. A bar or bat mitzvah has adult responsibilities under Jewish law. This might be the clue to the relative maturity and success of the Jewish young adult. They are encouraged to become conscious players in real life quite early but not before or without tutelage. They are not expected to live life instinctively without assistance and perspective.

Most traditional African societies also have their coming-of-age ceremonies at a similar life stage. According to Jewish law, young people are prepared, and when they attain the age of 13 (boys) and 12 (girls), they are deemed responsible for their actions and become sons and daughters of commandment and covenant: At this age, after intense teaching and instructions, the young ones are meant to become from thence personally responsible for Jewish law, tradition, and ethics.

Similarly, the African young adult went through the coming-of-age preparation and ceremony and emerged therefrom a man or woman, ready for the responsibilities that come with adulthood in his or her community. He or she would have had the mentoring and teaching needed to take on these responsibilities.

The West also had its own version of preparation when young ladies were sent to finishing schools and young men assigned to older relatives for mentoring and training. Unfortunately, these preparations have all but faded away with modernisation.

I was fortunate to have been blessed with the presence and impact of grandmothers especially. Some of the viewpoints and knowledge about aspects of life that I share in this book have not been learnt in formal education but significantly from the training and commentaries of my two grandmothers.

My maternal grandmother nurtured me in that critical first four years of life, and her influence continued, albeit from a distance, until she died in 2003. My paternal grandmother lived with my family during my preteen and early teenage years. She was a storyteller. Seeing she did not have the attention of our mum and dad, we children became her "captive audience." She spoke about diverse and grown-up topics and did wear us out as we could not see the relevance of some of her stories to our very young lives.

It is, however, amazing how much my sister and I to this day quote and remember her take on almost all matters. When I refer to my grandmother's take on a matter in the book, I mean either and both grandmothers because they have become one in my subconscious, and they both represent my roots.

I also got the gift of a very present, nurturing, and involved father. I believe I learnt most of what I know about active parenting and audacity of vision from him. My mother's main interest and preoccupation was keeping the hearth warm, and I have her to thank for teaching me domesticity.

Life tutelage based upon religion and culture can provide a good start and help in awakening one to the business of life; however, for a fulfilling and self-defined life of your dream, a level of consciousness is required of you, preferably from as early as possible, to make decisions and participate actively to achieve a planned and deliberate life. This book is therefore a clarion call and encouragement to consciousness and deliberateness in living the life one would be proud of in the end. It is a summary of the lessons I have learnt from my own life with its unique combination of circumstances and opportunities and of the books and other resources I have used in my quest for answers on the subject of life.

The work has been immensely contributed to by my observation of lives from both afar and close-up when I have been trusted and let into the lives of people I have counselled or coached. However, this is not a how-to book, because we each have our different and distinct paths. It is rather an attempt to bring into your consciousness the careful consideration and planning that the different aspects of life need on your own particular journey.

Due to my personal viewpoint of the relative importance of certain aspects of life to the success of the whole, the reader will find some chapters longer than others. I therefore declare my bias to the issues pertaining to parenting and financial security. Conversely, my opinion is that while a career, for example, would be a major differentiating aspect in life, the matter of careers and livelihood tend to loom large and want to crowd out 'softer' but equally critical aspects of life like parenting or relationships.

I hope, beyond all else, that the readers, in living more consciously, are not among the numbers who wake up one day and find that life has happened while they were not looking! The book must not be read in a particular sequence; it is arranged to allow you go to particular chapters or aspects as required by your particular stage, situation, or need for counsel at different times. The chapters are arranged based on the different stages and aspects of life, signposting the road junctions and timelines that the reader can expect to navigate on the journey of life. Different chapters will therefore be more applicable and enlightening for different readers at different times. It could be growing up and career-building time for some, marriage and parenting for others. It might be about manoeuvring middle and old age for yet another.

My hope is that you consciously navigate the boat of life, choose your desired outcomes, and formulate strategies to get there; that you own your life and take responsibility for it. Life does not come with an owner's manual; it is up to each of us to make the best of life as it unfolds.

According to American humorist Josh Billings, "Life consists not in holding good cards but in playing those you hold well".

'When it comes to what your life brings

It's all about your thoughts

You can blame the universe for being unfair

and find comfort in idea of victim hood

Ultimately it is all about you and how you

wear the choices presented to you by yourself

So take responsibility for the results

No matter if you like it or not.'

— Anonymous

Finally, my greatest motivation for writing this book, which kept me writing to the end, is my intention to be an impactful grandmother to my own grandchildren, through these 'conversations' with them, the way my own impacted me. Therefore, my dear grandchild, it is my love and concern for you, even while you are yet unborn, and my strong intention that you learn about critical aspects of life before you have to experience them that propels me to write. I write because I know I am most unlikely to be an in situ grandma to you, the way I experienced my own grandmothers, but I am sure we shall find our own times. Despite the wonderful upbringing that I am sure your parents are giving you, I need you to get this grandma's take on things.

After all, I have been here longer than your parents and have seen things play out longer than they have. Also, I am no longer overwhelmed by career and many things that occupy life at their age, so I am more ready to 'sit and talk' to you for as long as you will let me. As we might not even be living in the same location, most of our communication is likely to be by whatever is the current cool way of talking. But this book, shall always be unto you, the reference to what I think of the many perplexing stages and situations of life. Of course, it would give me endless joy if, as you read, you feel the need to call me for further clarifications, and then we can really talk!

In the end, no one can control all aspects of life all of the time, but you can be awake and write your own story by making things happen instead of just waiting and watching them happen or accepting whatever life brings. Make your life happen.

Acknowledgements

A Conscious Life is a special project that took five years to accomplish. For the idea to write this book, the enablement and all the help that I received, and of course for my unique combination of circumstances and opportunities, I have God to thank.

For their nurturing, cultural location and teaching, and, mostly, for their love, I am grateful to and celebrate my grandmothers, Raliat Salami and Ibidun Majaro. To my departed father, Lateef Ajibade Salami, for being my talk buddy, cheerleader, and bold visionary, love always. I thank my mother, Ajibike Salami, for dedicating so much of her life to tending to our family.

Special thanks to my husband, Femi, for reading the very first draft and returning an encouraging verdict. I also thank my sons for taking time from their frenetic work schedules to read the drafts of the first few chapters in their rawest form, and affirming that the project is worthwhile; you guys know how important your opinion is to me!

I am ever so grateful to those of you who encouraged me, some not so gently, to write and to finish: Sandra Cumming, who thought the book was a terrific idea; Wale Adefarasin, always gently nudging and finally endorsed the book; Barbara Lawrence for finding me a publisher; and Bisi Ogunko, my sister and believing cheerleader.

For insisting I write the book in my own peculiar voice with real-life examples and experience, I thank Laolu Adefarasin; and thanks to Singto Saro-Wiwa, who took me through the tedious discipline of chapter synopsis and structure right at the beginning!

I acknowledge, with heartfelt gratitude, the painstaking review of the book by Chief Ajibola Ogunshola and for turning in a concise but complete forward to the book; also to Shola Borha for reading and endorsing the book with her commentaries that make me proud to have made the effort.

On the path of life I have been lucky to come across people, too many to list here for a lack of space, who have, knowingly or unknowing, positively impacted my journey. I thank only a few such people here for their particular help while I wrote. Mrs Laide Sasegbon first taught me in school more than fifty years ago but remains my friend and teacher; she has held me so kindly on occasions when 'life happened' and I was bewildered; thanks, Auntie.

In Mr Ayo Olagundoye I found an unlikely philosophy enthusiast, having been a banker all his professional life. He kindly made time to discuss with me over coffee the application of philosophy to everyday living; many thanks.

To Pamela and Fela, my friends who gave me permission to use their real-life stories and experience to bring realness in discussing some aspects of life; thank you, girls!

I acknowledge the works of other people in the form of books and articles that I have read, learnt from and which might have encouraged me to write. Thank you all for spreading knowledge.

Finally, I am deeply grateful to my publishing consultant Gabriel Both, for his advice and suggestions that have brought great improvement to this edition of the book.

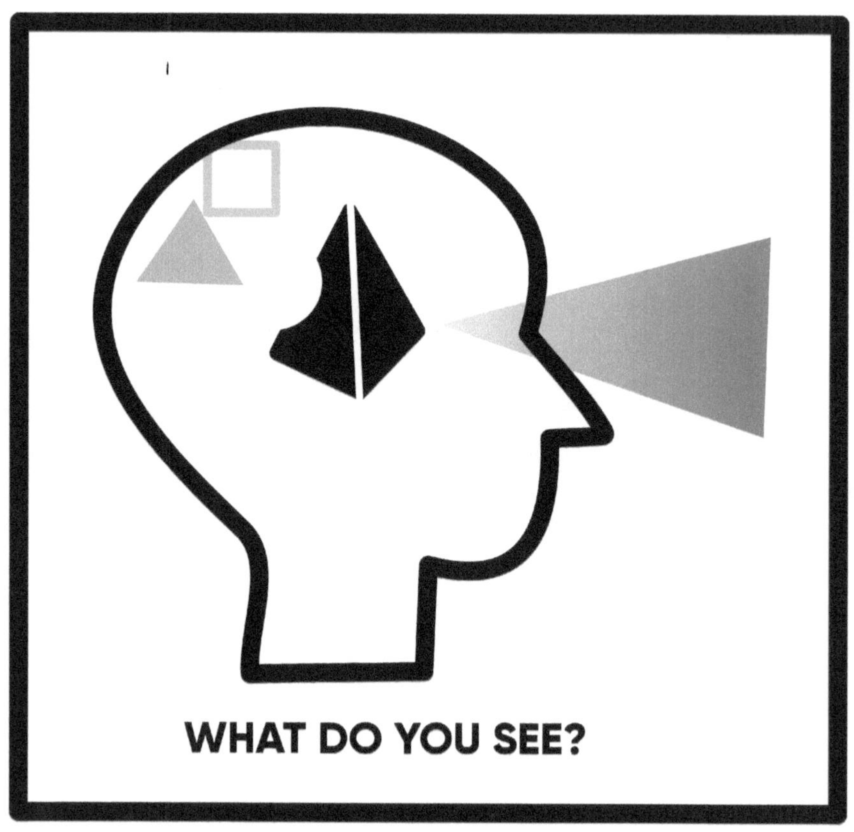
WHAT DO YOU SEE?

Chapter 1 - A Vision for Life

'The life truly worth living is the considered life.'

—Socrates

A number of us graduated between 1977 and 1980 depending on our course of study, with the medics taking almost forever, but we all landed our first jobs by 1981. One person appeared the luckiest of us all. He had bagged this incredible job that had him chauffeur driven and housed in a company accommodation right from that first rung. He was his own boss – at least that's what we believed – since he was the head of a regional office in a job with very good prospects. His very spacious home was the default hangout in the evenings and the party place on the weekends! I do not know if these seeming advantages made him less hungry than the rest of us in seeking progress. What was there to progress to when you are 25 and in his shoes?

In hindsight, I do not recall much in the way of the rest of us contributing to the cost of parties and hanging out, so we all must have been squandering a good chunk of his pay packet.

Then, life slowly began to happen; his long-time girlfriend got pregnant and had their first child. For some reason, and I sincerely hope we were not all part of the reason he was unwilling to yield his 'big-man party sponsor' status to settling down to boring domesticity, he would not marry her and had no reasonable excuse to proffer.

As can happen sometimes, when it rains, it pours – the unspeakable happened about a year into his situation. His hitherto invisible boss queried his work ethic and his unduly large office expenses, and our friend was too proud to be submissive and change his ways. He was not fired. He actually resigned in a huff of anger and arrogance. This person was definitely blessed with good opportunity early in life. However, he had no awareness of his good fortune, so he wasted and lost it.

By this time most of us were popping up with babies. And between sleepless nights of early parenting and rookie duties at work or with some form of self-development endeavour in postgraduate studies to differentiate our careers, there was little time left for partying. So we did not miss the departure of the party venue that went with his job.

Fast forward ten years. Because this person could not settle into another starter job since he had acquired the 'boss mentality', he job-hopped for a bit with no career progress. His personal life took on a pattern of moving through different female liaisons, such that there was always a new fiancée or live-in. This period culminated with him becoming a businessman of no specific business; he had a different exciting project on his plate each time we met and talked. And to complicate matters, a few children fathered by him with different mothers became part of his life's landscape.

Today, more than thirty years after that brilliant start, we all don't know where the years have gone – and seemingly so quickly! This person has become a pitiful shadow of the boy that had it all handed to him back then. No career ever happened, no project ever left the drawing board, and no organized family life delighted him. He, however, remains supportive of his friends, and you can always count on him to show up when showing up is required; he appears not to be too resentful of the leaps and bounds that others have achieved in their careers and family lives. If he feels any shame or resentment, it's apparently not enough for him to stay away from his childhood friends.

If you are thinking that most youngsters do not consciously plan the next thirty years when just out of college, you're not far from the truth. It's true that the kind of early opportunity he had is not common; most youngsters have the blessing of not much choice but to just get on with their starter jobs, raise a family, and begin self-development through further education. Planning and working towards the short-term goals of rent and parenting expenses is what most young people do. But I ask you, how much better would it be if you are able to have a long-term view and consciously plan for longer timelines and larger dreams from the get-go? How much better would it be to be aware so that you are able to recognise your dreams if an early opportunity rolls by and not let it roll away from your hands?

Taking Charge of Your Life

By quote at the chapter opening, I believe the philosopher, in seeking the best way to live, meant a life that is well informed, has worthwhile goals, and is lived discerningly and consciously with attention.

The State of Consciousness

As the word *conscious* forms part of the title, let us consider the concept of consciousness for a moment. By definition, consciousness is the understanding of the concept of self, or the executive control system of the mind. Consciousness typically implies subjectivity and selectivity.

My own favourite depiction of consciousness for the purpose at hand is the philosopher Franz Brentano's short definition: *intentionality* or *aboutness*. Intentionality and selectivity indicate the presence of intentions and the choosing of expected outcomes, respectively, while aboutness suggests preoccupation with doing something about those intentions. A conscious life can therefore be summed up from this definition as a life lived with intentionality towards selected outcomes with a good dose of aboutness.

Living consciously is living a life that is subject to the control of the person who lives it; it is about living as a person who actively experiences its passage with wakefulness and awareness. Also, it suggests a commitment to the idea of a self that needs to be tended with care and effort over time. It would require you to take an executive role in tending and creating that self that you desire to be and are committed to being. If you have certain intentions and expectations of your life, it is most likely that you would put some work and aboutness to the achievement of those intended outcomes. That would be a conscious life, intentionally lived.

If I am calling you to consciousness, there must be a possibility of living a life unconsciously and letting time pass with little or no intentions or expectations. Unconsciousness, in the medical sense, means being in a coma or in a state of helplessness. This might sound severe, but that is simply the opposite of consciousness. Also, we all have unconscious moments when we sleep or are instinctual even if awake. Such unconscious moments are however not ideal for doing anything to the best of one's ability – in this case, living life. The possibility that it however happens, harsh as it might sound, is evidenced by the disproportionately large number of people who appear to lack clarity of direction and purpose when you consider their behaviour and actions (or inactions, for that matter). Their confusion, lethargy and sometimes anguish in charting a path is often voiced during counselling and coaching sessions. Their struggle to find their ways in many aspects of life is usually palpable.

I have found that in the search for direction, what is of utmost importance but is regularly missed is the concept of *being* – being the person who undergirds all our doings. It is a common mistake for people to focus their lives on the doing and having while neglecting the being. So the question, actually, ought to be, who do you want to become? In the end it is not what you do but who you are that is most important and defining. By focussing first on who you are and who you want to become, to imagine what you would like to do and what you would like to have becomes a logical step. In the end, who you are and who you are becoming dictate what you are able to do and have. A disciplined person can put in the hours to build a robust business and thereby reap financial rewards. A compassionate person can see other people's needs for help and therefore provide such help.

But back to the question of who is in charge of your life. The answer would have to be that the one who decides who you want to become and where you are headed in life is the one in charge of your life. Your first step toward living a conscious life would have to be your accep tance and ownership of the responsibility of being in charge of your own life – to decide who your self should be, where that self is headed, and what needs to be done to get there. When you accept this responsibility and begin to act accordingly, choices get much easier. We live in a world of many distractions, multiple-choice situations, and dilemmas. If you try to figure things out as situations present themselves, life can become staccato in form and lead to nowhere in particular. But when your values, priorities, vision and purpose are clear – and you can easily remind yourself of these every day – then life's events and struggles are much easier to handle. Your choices will be easier to make, and life will be more orderly.

The truth is that we each evolve, day by day, year by year. You are, inevitably, becoming something and someone new all the time. You are not the same person you were a year or even six months ago. You know things you didn't know back then. You now have skills you didn't have.

Over time, we evolve. That evolution either happens by accident or on purpose, either as a result of life's random events or resulting from the choices you make, according to a plan you are consciously following. Every day provides a chance for another small step in that direction.

In the end, while many people and events will influence you, you can be in charge of your own evolution. My take is that you have a better chance of becoming that person and living the life you desire if your life evolves on purpose. Imagine what astounding results can be achieved if you resolve to be in the driver's seat, to create the person and future you truly desire. A life in which its evolution is self-directed and self-propelled in a deliberate, wilful, and consistent manner is sure to amount to much. In other words, you are *taking charge*. You can really be in charge if you pay attention, commit to a conscious life, and deliberately live it.

The miracle is that you can change to consciousness and intentional living at any stage of life. If you start having intentions of thought, the desired outcomes will follow. Our thoughts have been proven to be the genesis and causal influence of our goals. You can have intentions about the kind of thoughts you wish to think. What we think paints the image of our desired outcomes long before they manifest and not to intentionally direct our thoughts make the future hazy. In the intervening period, our actions are inevitably influenced by those thoughts in the direction of those outcomes. Over time, the result of our intentions of thoughts and actions is the manifestation of those outcomes.

The secret to achieving these outcomes is to begin to take intentional actions towards them. There is no point in having intentions in thought without making the effort and taking actions towards them. Nothing that is worthwhile has not been consciously or intentionally desired and worked for. It is in consistently reminding yourself to take those actions that you get into the habit of conscious living and bearing fruits. No one who has achieved a worthwhile thing is surprised at achieving it because he or she would usually have desired it and made the effort to get it.

I know, more than most people, judging by my own experiences, that you cannot plan for all external factors and that life does deal an unexpected hand now and again. However, a defined set of values and desired outcomes to which you are consciously committed and pursuing ensures your reaction to such 'surprises' are somewhat controlled and the distraction does not take you too far from your course or even make you abandon your mission. This is why some people appear better grounded and not overwhelmed or swept away by occasional storms. They ride out the storms better because they are able to focus on their defined destination. As in all manners of planning, you should be ready for deviations from your life plan, but the achievements from a planned life lived consciously, even with such deviations, are astounding when compared to one left entirely to chance.

Who's in Charge Anyway?

What would your answer be if you were asked the question, who is in charge of the paths and outcomes of your life? I suspect you might give various answers that suggest you hold other people – your parents, your spouse, your boss, or even the government – responsible for how your life has played out so far and how it will in the future. The divine definitely cannot deny playing some role here; after all, we had no say in when, where, and to whom we were born, and none of us can recall voting in the election to decide if we should even ever have been born at all! However, this is an all-important question that seeks answers about your personal life, your work life, your values, and your spirituality, as well as the really big goals and dreams of your life. It is a question that makes you consider and participate in who you are becoming, where you are headed in life, and what you and other people might be doing or need to start doing to get to a desirable end.

Who Is Your Self

The first step to your commitment to a conscious life is understanding the concept of self and accepting that you can choose to take control over that self. Understanding this helps you realise that life is, for the most part, not a family journey. It brings to realisation the exciting fact that you are unique from even an identical twin. You are able to acknowledge and accept the attributes and talents that differentiate you from all others and be motivated to work without hesitation with those attributes for your best. With this freedom you can truly define who you want that self to be, developing a very clear picture of the personality that you aspire to. This can happen at any stage of life, depending on when you finally take the responsibility to be in charge of yourself, but the earlier it happens the better, so you can bring some intentionality to letting your desired life begin to manifest. A detailed definition of that self is most likely to be derived in stages, almost like a rolling plan, whereby the details can only be realistically created for limited periods of time into the future.

However, there should be a clear idea of the general direction you are headed. It seems to me that while Barack Obama might not have had the audacity to seriously believe he would become president of the United States right after his first college degree, if one connected the dots of his life as depicted in his book *Dreams of My Father*, it was clear that he wanted more than the ordinary and was willing to sacrifice for it. He got involved with community organising, which might not have been the most lucrative, glamorous, or logical career direction for him at the time. According to his wife, Michelle, when asked by a schoolgirl during their state visit to the United Kingdom if she ever imagined he would become president, she replied that she could not have imagined it but that she always knew he would be a very useful person. In other words, she saw some evidence of 'aboutness' in the young Barack that meant or represented usefulness to her even back then.

The question you ought to ask yourself is whether a bystander can detect some evidence of what you are about from the way you go about your life.

A Defined Self Is Your Brand

A defined self can be likened to a brand. A brand is a particular kind or variety of a product with an identifying mark. Brand expert Tom Peters says you are a brand, and you are in charge of your brand. Your personal brand is based on the list of characteristics that make you most likely to achieve the life you have chosen. Once your brand is carefully selected, defined, and fully committed to, it becomes automatic for you to intentionally portray and maintain the brand, also to consciously abstain from actions that might undermine or damage it. My grandmother was adamant that the reason it was important that we behaved and talked sensibly in public was to avoid damaging her own brand as the grandmother who trained her grandchildren well.

Your brand can evolve over time as a result of the values and experiences of your childhood or can be consciously developed as life unfolds. It should echo what you believe, do best like no other can, and thereby build up expectations of others on which you must deliver. A teacher in a schoolroom knows the student who would promptly hand in a well-researched assignment as well as the student who is bound to be involved with any disturbances in class, and these are forms of branding at an early stage in life. A good brand should command respect and loyalty. Other people who consider your brand desirable should respect you and wish to associate with you.

Understanding commitments helps to create and maintain a personal brand. Constantly considering commitments to family, community, and ultimately to yourself and delivering on them is what makes a personal brand strong. In my small circle of family and friends, I recognise personal brands and rely on the promise of each. I turn to my 'nurturing homemaker' friend when I need help with sourcing food and other home provisions. When I need to be firmly set aright about an important matter, knowing well in advance that the advice I am likely to get would be a difficult pill to swallow, I go to my 'ever rational, wise, and brick-wall' friend. And on the occasions that I need encouragement, affirmation, and a lift in my spirit, I know just the right number to dial.

Any owner of a great brand will attest that maintaining it can be a bigger challenge than defining and building it. You must protect the integrity of your brand. Actions or pronouncements that could cause irreversible damage to the brand must be avoided. Ultimately, it is through the effort of maintaining your brand that you form the habits that ensure the achievement of your vision, so brand maintenance is key.

How Early Can You Take Charge?

Apparently, different people take charge at different chronological ages. However, the earlier you're able to snap into the consciousness of your responsibility for achieving the outcomes you desire, the better. Living a conscious life can be compared to saving towards a sum of money: the earlier you start, and the more momentum you give your savings, the earlier your target sum can be reached. Unfortunately, the later you start consciously managing your life, the more likely your chances of making early mistakes that could have lifelong implications. Dropping out of college before becoming conscious, for example, would slow down the process of becoming that person you finally desire to become if that college degree is critical to the self you defined. So if you have still not answered the question of who is in charge of your life, there it is: you ultimately are! The saying 'failing to plan is planning to fail' has no stronger implication than in a life allowed to drift unconsciously for too long.

Creating a Vision for Your Life—Where Are You Headed?

'For imagination sets the goal 'picture' on which our automatic mechanism works on. We act, or fail to act, not because of 'will', as is so commonly believed, but because of imagination.'

—Maxwell Maltz

Imagination plays a big role in defining the life a person truly wants. When author Stephen Covey talks about "starting with the end in mind", he means having a vision of the outcome. It is one thing to talk about written goals, but those goals can only be born of vivid imaginations. You must be able to imagine what you consider a great life in order to aspire to it; you must know what features make this particular life desirable. These could be the desired contents – say, a nurturing family life – or the absence of undesirable elements, like financial disorder. According to the Maltz quote above, our ability or failure to take action is not always due to a lack of will but for lack of a goal or vision on which our automatic mechanism can work. The human automatic mechanism is the reliance of human emotions and actions on what vision or goal picture is fed into the mind.

Man has no automatic knowledge and can have no automatic values. We are born with an emotional mechanism, but at birth it is *tabula rasa.* Your emotional mechanism at birth is like an electronic computer which has no program, and its subsequent programming consists of the values your mind chooses. You choose your emotional values by a conscious process of thought or accept them by default through subconscious associations, on faith, on someone's authority, or blind imitation. Little wonder then that the Christian Bible says a people perish for lack of a vision! The forty years it took the people of Israel to arrive in the Promised Land was not due to a long distance (apparently, they had quite a few merry-go-rounds because they had no idea what their destination would look like); it was either as a result of failure to conjure up the vision of the desired destination or by conjuring wrong based on the authority of the advance look-out parties who gave them dreadful reports about the place! So rather than consciously build their own vision, according to Ayn Rand, they must have subconsciously accepted the report of the spies based on faith in their authority! Unfortunately, blindly following another happens so often in life.

Imagining starts in the mind. The quality of thinking that supports imagination is understandably not a walk in the park, but it is a most critical ingredient for a charted life. It is the process from which dreams and visions evolve, and without dreams and visions, extraordinary feats are unlikely. Picasso probably didn't start out with visions of how financially valuable his paintings would become, but he must have imagined the beauty he wished to create before starting each masterpiece.

Harnessing your thoughts for constructive imagination is difficult at the most tranquil of times, much less so in a chaotic world of constant information and distraction by social media. It's so easy to become too lazy or distracted to envision the specifics we want for a fulfilling life or get held back by the fear of imagined failure. For whichever reason, you must not deny yourself a framework to work within and a target to keep 'shooting' at. You must not make yourself become more prone to distractions, meandering, and a general lack of purpose; number yourself with the disciplined few who are able to think up a plan for the future, and you will easily be one of life's outliers. The few who positively stand out from the average masses.

Living the Life You Desire Intentionally.

Having learnt that anyone can create and live a great life, you still need certain skills and a lot of discipline to actually achieve it. In the hope that you are now enthused to take up the mantle of consciousness and a sense of self to envision the life you adjudge as great, and to build a personal brand that can achieve such a life, I'm sorry to now tell you that all of that is not enough! You actually have to face the many days in each year and the many years in your future, living them according to the tenets and values of your personal brand and vision.

Trust me: a wonderful life does not 'just happen' because you envisioned it. It is not luck or chance that makes good things happen while keeping the bad aspects of life to a minimum. However, a life of peace, passion, purpose, and fulfilment is not the result of unusual intelligence, education, having the right parents, or even a good job. Rather, a great life is like a tapestry, carefully sewn with attention and dedication over time. It's the result of doing the right things, in the right way, at the right time, over and over again. And it requires the discipline to avoid doing the wrong things that are so tempting at most times. The good news is that anyone can learn this discipline, but it is intriguing that so few make the effort.

There are some fundamental principles that I have found to make life come together well. I am hoping these become your mantras of the kind I am infamous for with my children. Without realising it, I apparently constantly start giving my take on most matters by saying, "As my grandmother would say", or "As the Yoruba would say".

These principles are required in all aspects of life, be it in work and career, marriage, parenting, or maintaining a healthy lifestyle.

The Everyday Things and Temptations—Persistent Self-Discipline

'You must do the things today that others will not do so that you can have the things tomorrow that others will not have.'

—Author unknown

My experience is that a conscious and disciplined life is actually easier and more convenient than a life of disorder and frustration. I see a great life as the result of earnestly addressing life's everyday things when it is tempting to procrastinate and avoid actively engaging the situations. Conversely, life's pitfalls are the predictable results of giving in to the little temptations that seem so attractive in the moment. A great and healthy body can be achieved by the discipline of regular exercise, while constantly feeding the body with the little temptations of chocolate, alcohol, and fast food will, in all probability, result in a mammoth body size and an increased probability of debilitating illnesses! Also, finding the time and commitment to feed your mind with good and edifying activities will produce a very different outcome from endless hours spent surfing the Internet for corrupting material. It is profitable wisdom to pay attention to the everyday things and watch out for the little temptations! You need to be consistent in doing the profitable things and disciplined enough in surmounting the little temptations.

A conscious life demands that you do the things most people can't be bothered to do, that you go the extra mile. A great life does not preclude recreation and having a good time, but when work and diligence are called for, you are required to do the right things in the right way, and in a timely manner. Ultimately, it is the matching of your vision with personal discipline and determination that results in worthwhile achievements.

Periodic Review of Roadmaps, Deadlines, and Destinations

'A dream is just a dream. A goal is a dream with a plan and a deadline.'

—Harvey Mackay

It is critical that you stop periodically and carry out an honest review of your life. Many people are reminded to do an annual exercise towards the end of each year for the New Year resolutions. I prefer my six-month reviews, which keep me on my toes and ensure I can pull back before I go too far down a wrong road. Periodical reviews allow you consider your progress against set deadlines and destinations. Each time you focus on your set goals vis-à-vis the current state of play, that point in time becomes the baseline of the rest of your life from where to regroup for the task ahead. The future is unknown for the most part, but every day is a new chance to redirect life. As the ancient Chinese proverb says, "The best time to plant a tree is twenty years ago. The second best time is now".

During such reviews, think through the roadmap and the actions still required to reach your goals or destinations. You should be spurred on to start taking such identified actions rather than leave them for some indeterminable future. In different aspects of life, your goals should be seen as destinations. some intermediate, leading to the final ones. Intermediate destinations help break down plans to easier achievable subsets that make the journey not seem endless, which could cause weariness, if not outright abandonment of expedition. The ambition of a teenager to become a medical doctor, for example, is better managed by concentrating in the meantime on studying the right subjects in school. The intermediate destination becomes the achievement of requisite grades in those subjects. Regular review of intermediate goals will also ensure they remain the optimum route to the final destination. Finally, deadlines must be set for arriving at each destination for discipline. A dream only becomes a goal if there is a plan to achieve it within a set deadline.

Be Careful of Past Impacts That Continue to Influence Your Life

'We can chart our future clearly and wisely only when we know the path which has led to the present.'

—Adlai Stevenson

All of us, even if not always conscious of it, are influenced by some impact or combination thereof in the form of culture, society, people, or events at different times. These impacts are the reason we think and act the way we do and sometimes beyond our natural temperament react to situations in a specific manner. You will find that sometimes two people exposed to the same situations are not necessarily influenced in the same way or intensity. This might be due to a difference in their natural temperaments or in their conscious choice of how they would be influenced by the event. For example, two children of a divorce might grow up to approach marriage very differently. While one may find it a challenge to stay committed in relationships because of this experience, thereby re-enacting the malfunction of their childhood experience, the other might become an adult that would do everything and anything to achieve a stable family life.

It is very useful to be able to identify the impacts of your past and remain aware of their continuing influence. Its import is in ensuring the lessons from your past are not wasted while consciously reinforcing the positive influences. On the other hand, it is crucial that the affectations and influences of any negative impacts are dealt with to avoid their influence marring your future. To this end, it would be of immense help if the negatively impacted of the two children in the divorce example sought counselling help to relearn security and commitment in marriage. We are each a tapestry of our past influences. With attention to and deliberate management, the tapestry can be a beautiful backdrop to a happy future.

A person living life consciously must in turn take seriously the responsibility for the impacts he or she is exposed to. Intentionally exposing yourself to a person or situation should usually be because a positive influence is sought, as would be the case in a mentoring situation. However, it is common to see people being unknowingly impacted! It behoves you to be watchful for negative impacts that are sometimes not easily discernible, such as in friendships and associations. It is your duty to yourself once the possibility of such negative impacts is identified to actively remove yourself from the path of damage. On the other hand, the possibility of your being an impact on others places a responsibility on you. As friend, teacher, mentor, parent, or even neighbour, you could be unknowingly impacting some impressionable others, so you need to consciously endeavour to remain a positive influence.

The lessons from the 2008 British drama film *Slumdog Millionaire* about impacts on life were glaring. The fact that the same experience can have different impacts and outcomes on two people was shown through the different lives of two brothers raised in a slum. While one brother naturally settled into a life of crime, which ultimately destroyed him, the other appeared to have lived a conscious life despite his surroundings, which prepared him to become a millionaire. All of his knowledge in the competition that won him a million dollars showed that there are learning opportunities in all life experiences if one pays attention. He apparently had a clear idea of self and kept faith with his core values, which helped him to ultimately use his life lessons to excel. The same impacts were the excuse the other brother used to self-destruct. How we are impacted by situations is really up to us and our sense of self.

You must Acquire the Skills to Inhabit Your Desired Life

You must include in your plans ways of acquiring the skills and know-how, apart from formal education, to fit your desired lifestyle. The life in which you are fulfilled and proud requires that you meet its demands with some confidence and grace. Learn what you need to know to inhabit your desired position in life with confidence. Read good materials. Get a coach or mentor if necessary. Mimic the people who are already in those positions, and befriend them if possible. While some might consider this thirst to be your preferred self as social pretences, I see it as a prerequisite for upward social mobility. You should be able to aspire to nobility and grace if that is what is attractive to you and would make you proud, and you should make no apologies for it.

Imbibe Excellence in All Things

Having the presence of mind to maintain extremely high standards in all you do has a cumulative effect that produces recognition and personal fulfilment over time. This means doing your work to a high standard, paying attention to your appearance through grooming, watching your money habits, taking care of your health, making good life decisions, treating other people well, and insisting that they treat you as you wish to be treated. After a while a habit of excellence is formed. The results are usually outstanding. No one can prevent you from defining, creating, and living the life you desire, but a fulfilling life does require something of you. It requires a plan, excellent standards, good tools, and the discipline to live the life you desire. It requires that you remain conscious in living it.

In the end, the key message is that you ought to have a clear vision of the life you consider fulfilling and of which you would be proud.

Chapter 2 – Growing Up: Childhood and Young Adulthood

I came across a young man through his wife, who had requested marriage counselling. I met this soft-spoken and seemingly enviable man in his late thirties with a good career and married to a similarly accomplished wife. He appeared the perfect gentleman, and they were blessed with three lovely children and lived in an upmarket part of town. It was the dark side of their family life that brought the wife to counselling. He had become an abusive husband and father; nobody was safe after one of his drinking sprees, and his wife's body bore the marks as evidence. When he finally agreed to submit himself to counselling, it was soon found that the source of his demons was from his childhood. He was the only child of a single mother who moved from one live-in liaison to another during his growing-up years. He saw and heard abuse in different forms over his childhood, and despite good performances in school and career, the demons from his past continued to plague him, and he found an outlet in alcohol and violent abuse of his loved ones. Unfortunately, the scarring of his childhood was not only proving destructive to his adult life, because without help, his children's experiences would negatively influence their own lives in the future.

This opening quote reminds us that there are indeed different seasons to life, and each season can exemplify a particular attitude, say folly in youth and, commonly, remorse at old age. Childhood, during which a person is most impressionable, should be deliberately nurtured to ensure later life is not characterised by demons from the past and remorse. That we are particularly impacted by the childhood stage of life is the reason to recall how yours went and pay particular attention when you have the responsibility of nurturing a child. Furthermore, it is useful to bring consciousness to how you intend to navigate the different stages of life and the transition from one to the next. The opportunities and abilities of each stage differ, and missing those at any stage is regretful as they can have very long term effects far into full adulthood.

Whether you are a young adult or already in the season of parenthood, the intention is to emphasize the importance of managing what are crucial stages in human development, the ways childhood and young adulthood can influence the rest of your life. The hope is that younger readers are encouraged to be conscious in what they do because of possible future effects, and adult readers are made more reflective, first of their own childhood to gain a better understanding of the contribution of that to who they are today, as well as how they impact the lives of the children entrusted to them.

> *'What we remember from childhood we remember forever: permanent ghosts, stamped inked, imprinted, eternally seen.'*
>
> —Cynthia Ozick

That we are substantially shaped from childhood and retain details and influences from that season of life I personally can testify to. Half a century later I have flashbacks from my early childhood, sometimes very vivid. Some of the events that I remember both their details and fallout happened when I could not have been older than 5 at the time. This makes me know that there are in each of us deep roots of our childhood with continuing influence in adulthood. Adults would do well not to expose children to damaging traumatic events if it can be helped, and if it cannot be helped, to make efforts to mitigate the lasting impact. Children actually do see, hear, and remember much more than adults give them credit for!

Reflecting on Your Childhood Experiences

Reflecting on your childhood as an adult will help identify influences from that critical period that need understanding and attention if they were not to undermine your future. It is also worthwhile to take an interest in the childhood experiences of people that you seek to forge a close bond with – a spouse, for example.

In looking back into the memories of your childhood, understanding how particular circumstances formed you, and how the society of your youth regarded and treated children, you would gain a better understanding of the resulting and continuing influence. If, say, you were raised in a more traditional setting, where the 'village' raised all the children and the family extended beyond the nuclear to layers of cousins, uncles, and aunties, then you are likely to view very differently, for example, the matter of extended family involvement from a spouse who might have experienced childhood in a strictly nuclear sense. This enlightenment would bring a mutual understanding and could forestall crises arising from a difference in attitudes in this area.

I recall a very happy time with my maternal grandparents in the first five years of my childhood. I also recall that I was taken to school early at about the age of 3, long before the registration age of 5, because a relative taught kindergarten, so I sat in her class without registration. I do believe this early exposure to learning and the public left a foundation of self-motivation and confidence from which I still draw on today. I clearly recollect the stories by my paternal grandmother during the impressionable segment of my youth (between ages 9 and 13). The storyteller that she was shared her real-life stories with us children, and it is amazing how lastingly influencing some of the biases and mind-sets she laid down with those stories have proven to be. My grown-up sons have been handed down my grandmotherly opinion about every possible situation or topic, and those opinions happen to remain relevant even now.

While we cannot help the incidence and circumstances of our birth and childhood, it is a worthwhile exercise to look back into our memories of its facts and influences. A reflection of your childhood can help identify foundational influences from that critical period; some of those are for good and can enrich life while some need to be better understood and dealt with if they are not to undermine a successful life.

A deep reflection of your childhood is a responsibility you owe yourself to better understand your tendencies and what in your childhood could have laid the foundation for those tendencies. The application of this understanding to your current and future experiences would make for a more deliberately lived life and avoidance of pitfalls due to the past. Hopefully, the knowledge will in turn make you more thoughtful in impacting the life of a child that falls under your influence.

Adult Responsibilities for Childhood

It can be safely concluded that the responsibility for childhood lies mainly with adults, at least until after puberty when the child should begin to develop some self-consciousness. Any adult who is responsible for children ought to be in constant thought about the long-term effects of their actions and the guidance they provide to ensure a smooth transition from childhood to young adulthood.

Although the socioeconomic background of parents has an obvious effect on child development, what parents do with their children, even before they begin to talk, is found to be much more important. The indication is that children whose parents foster a loving communication achieve higher scores when they begin school than those who lack such opportunity. Furthermore, it is no surprise that children who attended preschool institutions and were involved in a wide range of developmental activities have several advantages over those with extended exposure to unsupervised television. In a higher income bracket family there can be as many as one per bedroom, which might actually be doing more harm than just a negative impact on family bonding! While traditional indicators such as material wealth remain influential in the quality of childhood because of the affordability of better education, for example, what you do with your children and how you communicate with them at that critical stage is far more important than expensive holidays and gifts. What is critical at childhood is that adults remain conscious and watchful of the stimuli and their effects that a child is exposed to at this life stage.

The following findings should help in guiding adults in nurturing children:

- Children who are held, hugged, and complimented end up being confident and loving adults.

- Discipline in childhood is critical. Discipline is not punishment. The Holy Bible encourages us to train up a child and when he is grown, he would not depart from the good way. Children whose chaotic energies are harnessed and positively controlled are being helped early to practice self-control and respect for other people. These are characteristics that will stand them in good stead for the rest of their lives.

- Security and the absence of violence in the home have a lasting effect on personal peace of mind and emotional stability for children leading into adulthood.

- Adolescents that are lovingly supported and directed stand a better chance of gaining consciousness early and transitioning to adulthood with fewer crises.

The Sacredness of the Season of Childhood

All in all, an understanding of childhood and its long-term effect is needed if you are actively involved in managing and influencing this crucial stage of development, be it of your own children or wards in your sphere of influence. A child is not as helpless and totally dependent like an infant but remains a child even when he becomes the seemingly self-assured adolescent. Childhood can imply a varying range of ages, but it is safe to assume it begins after the first birthday when a child begins to speak and take first steps independently and ends after the turbulent adolescent years, at about 18.

In many societies it is expected that children are not responsible for themselves until after the 18th birthday, hence the reliance on the custodians and society to provide the support, guidance, and hopefully the conscious nurturing that would ensure a good childhood and strong foundation for the rest of a life.

The importance and sacredness of the period of childhood with its continuing influence through life cannot be overemphasised when the result of various scientific research also show that the period from infancy to the age of 3 is a critical time in child brain development that lays the neurological foundation for intellectual growth all the way to adolescence and adulthood. Most of the foundation for the physical and mental development of a person is laid in childhood. This is also the critical season for establishing good habits of both character and nutrition which can last a lifetime. Times have changed since when children were seen merely as the means of continuing the family line or just as an extension of the parents. Most societies now understand the importance of seeing the child as a beautiful and creative individual in his or her own right, albeit one whose chaotic energy needs to be harnessed and consciously directed.

Adolescence and Raging Hormones

Adolescence is the stage when the responsibility for consciously engaging with life ought to start in earnest. However, relative levels of readiness in different youngsters can be due to either nurture or nature. The sense of self at this stage can be helped by nurturing and direction by adults in a youngster's life. This is naturally a period of identity formation and self-definition which occurs between puberty at about age 12 and the age of maturity (18). The Latin word *adolescere*, the root word for adolescence, means 'to grow up', and it is hardly surprising that this stage is typified by a search for and insistence on self-identity which can be responsible for the turbulence felt by both the adolescent and the adult responsible for him or her. Adolescents really 'grow up' in size and attitude, usually all of a sudden.

It would be better if this need and search for identity is done when the adolescent has become conscious of and taken some responsibility for the life he or she wishes to live and bring this to bear in the struggle for self-definition and self-identity. Since this is also the last station of childhood when an adult is legally responsible for guiding, caring for, and making decisions for the adolescent, a healthy dose of understanding and patience is required at this stage on the adult's part if the effect of the raging hormones at puberty were not to constantly degenerate into full-blown war between them.

As an adolescent, it is understandable that you naturally want to establish your own identity, separate and distinct from your family, and you constantly feel misunderstood. It is, however, advisable that you begin to practice some self-control and have consideration for the long-term effects of your actions at this stage of life. You may experience some resentment of adult authority as you feel grown up enough to deserve independence and respect, but the important things to bear in mind are that

- adults usually have your best interest at heart;

- you do not have to do all your growing up in one fell swoop, as you are not equipped to do so anyway;

- undue aggression in putting your ideas across only makes your case look bad, resulting in a brick wall from the adult world;

- you must begin to understand and take a long-term view of your life to avoid taking actions that would impair it in the future (this might sound boring to you now); and

- you should try to identify some role models and mentors (the manager at your favourite nightclub or the much older neighbour considered the black sheep of his family don't count!). A good mentor should help you articulate and work towards the decent person you would like to be in future.

Young Adulthood: The Freedom before Settlement

For a variety of reasons, the timeline of young adulthood cannot be exactly defined; both social and individual variations make for a large grey area. However, a young adult is generally a person aged between 18 and 30. Arguably, with people living longer, going through education faster, age brackets for life stages have become pretty elastic. Despite all such fluidity, there is broad agreement that it is essentially the twenties and early thirties that constitute young adulthood – that period where you are not quite an adult but you have left your adolescent ways behind. After the identity search in adolescence, the young adult, in converse, actually tends to become eager and willing to fuse his identity with that of others and commit to affiliations and partnerships in the form of work and relationships, searching for his place in the world as he leaves home.

At this point in your life, as you choose your lifestyle and company, you need to be comfortable and confident in your own skin. Self-esteem can make a world of difference as you try to fuse into society. Your new surroundings and the loss of the emotional or financial security enjoyed at home can lead to complexes with far reaching consequences. Promiscuity, alcohol abuse, and use of drugs are common problems that could rear their heads as a result of damage to self-worth. Often, your relationship with your parents change somewhat; you may feel too old to live with them but might not be quite ready to live independently; therefore, as you try to form an identity as an individual apart from your family, it is usually stabilizing to keep ties with family no matter how fragile. If you do not, you would be losing a great support system both emotionally and economically. It is why this period has been described by sociologist Keneth Kenniston as the "time of extended economic and personal temporariness". While you might have left home, you are still a very long way from being ready for adult responsibilities. The worrisome thing I want to bring to your attention about this stage is that it is during this time of dramatic change and exploration that you must make crucial choices regarding education, work, marriage, family, and lifestyle. All these choices need to be made before you may in fact have the maturity or life experience to understand their seriousness in order to choose wisely. You need all the help you can get to acquire the maturity and experience needed to make these all important choices; be it in the form of advice from family and mentors, observation of role models, or training yourself through a conscious thought process and reading.

Sigmund Freud was right in saying young adulthood is a time for work and love. Your life would be most likely centred on career and relationships with the challenges that emanate therefrom, and this is the time you are expected to make all these decisions that will determine your future. You need to approach it with a sense of purpose as an investment into your own future! The challenges you are bound to encounter in doing this should be effectively engaged with rather than avoided or handled with fright, as you are likely to be living with the outcomes and consequences for the rest of your life.

The Age Thirty Transition and Settling Down

As early adulthood comes to a close around 28, when life starts to become more settled, then comes the onset of what the sociologist Daniel Levinson calls the age-30 crisis. Others have termed it 'the catch-30 passage'.

As the thirties approach, it is common for a young person to leave the life structure of the twenties, and to start anew, most of the time unconsciously, to create the basis for the next season of life. The age 30 transition can be a stressful one as the responsibilities of adult life in the form of work, mortgage, marriage, and maybe children loom large. Life suddenly appears too daunting, and you could experience a huge dose of self-doubt and anxiety.

This is the stage of life when, no matter how stressful it all seems, you need to keep swimming intentionally towards your many goals and all should fall in place as long as you keep applying the right principles to the different aspects of life. Fortunately, by the end of your thirties, a dividend should be noticeable from the financial and emotional investments you have made so far. You become more focused on advancing your career to its peak while gaining stability in your personal life and raising a family also take priority.

Mindful Navigation and Manoeuvring of The Transitions

Mindfully navigating, manoeuvring and actualizing these stages of life is at the core of living a satisfying life; it requires the attention of adults who have stewardship for raising children and the attention and deliberateness of young adults once they become self-aware to make right decisions to behave appropriately. Missing out on properly manoeuvring these stages of life could be the beginning of what is described as a life of quiet desperation that can degenerate to one of regret.

Seeing how childhood and young adulthood are crucial in laying down the roots which continue to influence your life for a long time, childhood should never be glossed over by parents as a time when real life is yet to commence; Neither should young adulthood be frittered away with unthinking youthful exuberance or rebellion by young adults. It is critical to stay as awake as you possibly can at these transitions for a life to harvest richly.

INTELLIGENCE
COACHING
WEBNARS
EDUCATION
DEVELOP YOUR MIND
3
A
COMMITMENT
GOALS
KNOWLEDGE
designed by freepik

Chapter 3 - Education and Learning

'Education is the passport to the future, for tomorrow belongs to those who prepare for it today.'

—Malcom X

The word education is derived from the Latin word *educere,* which means 'to bring out or bring forth what is within, or bring out potential'. Any act or experience that has a formative or improving effect on your mind, character, or physical ability educates you. It is through education that a society deliberately transmits its accumulated knowledge, skills, and value from one generation to another. Over time, this transmission evolved from the traditional oral teachings to what we now know as the schooling system. However, beyond schooling, education should be the process by which you learn and your full potential is brought forth. The education of your mind, character, and total person has to be beyond schooling as some aspects of education are simply not available there.

For potential to fully develop, all forms of learning that improve one over the lifetime should be considered education. Beyond the formal system of education lies a wide arena of learning and self-development that you should consider and employ to bring out your full personal potential. The strong correlation between knowledge and learning with personal and societal economics is a good reason for a person seeking to benefit society and be personally fulfilled to take learning seriously. You should constantly be aware of the learning opportunities that would help you achieve your set life goals, how you might obtain them, and how these might change as your life evolves. Continuous enlightenment and education should be a journey, not a destination. This is the only way to ensure none of your potential is wasted and life remains dynamic.

Formal Education—Conscious Direction and Planning

Generally, the education system, in which teachers are charged to direct the education of students, by drawing on a curriculum of subjects, delivers the prescribed education from toddlerhood to young adulthood in the preschool, primary, secondary, and tertiary stages.

We all know and approach schooling from the mandatory stance but the differentiating virtue is in the right choice of the right schools and subjects that would support our or our wards' desirable futures. It is the attention and consciousness you bring to the specific schooling needs and making the choice that best fits those needs that decide whether or not schooling is a preparation for a rewarding future.

Infant education lays a useful foundation of education for children before the commencement of obligatory education, usually between ages zero and 5 in the form of preschool, nursery, and playgroup. As this stage is when most of the child's brain development for future intellectual growth is laid, this is an important segment of education for a parent to pay particular attention to. Preschool should not be selected carelessly as an alternative to a nanny service; a preschool that is able to stimulate development in the child in a safe environment is critical. The quality and qualification of the teachers, as opposed to just being carers, must be high on the checklist of a parent considering a place for infant education.

No Sooner Are They Born than School Fees Are Due

Primary education is the first five or six years of structured education starting at the age of about five. This is followed by secondary schooling during adolescence with all the drama of that life-stage. The primary and secondary stages of schooling, being usually structured by authorised curriculums and stage examinations make them very straightforward and not easily lent to vagrancies. However, it is at this stage that the parent makes the choice between public funded education and fee-paying private education. While private schools are likely to deliver a wider education including a variety of extracurricular activities and exposure than the public funded schools, the later can provide just as sound education in most developed societies.

The gap between private and public funded education widens mostly in the developing world where underdevelopment and poverty might prevent effective public funding of education. A decision between public and private education is usually ultimately rested on affordability. It behoves a parent to make this decision early enough in order to adequately plan towards affording the education you consider best for your child. As part of your overall lifestyle and financial plan, size of family and income level are the two critical variables that are under your control in planning for the quality or type of education you desire for your children. It requires long term financial planning that naturally has an inbuilt notice period from the birth of each child. An education endowment fund from the get go is your best bet as the years do creep up on you. No sooner are they born than school fees are due!

Secondary education is the last segment of compulsory education for minors, after which a young adult has the option to elect to tertiary, or higher education at a university, polytechnic, or vocational college. It is crucial that the transition from secondary to selective higher education is consciously managed to ensure the student gravitates towards subjects he or she has talent and enthusiasm for.

While many parents are known to have their own ambitious preferences, they should be careful in angling for particular career goals for their children. Parents should only encourage and help their children to study subjects that keep their career goal choices open and in line with their talents. This is critical at the stage of meeting entry requirements for study at the tertiary stage. The chances for success in tertiary study and future career are greatly helped when 'round pegs are in round holes' and subjects studied at secondary school stage keep good options open for the right placement in a tertiary institution. The tertiary stage is where students are taught with a view towards preparing them with specific knowledge, skills, or abilities that can be applied upon completion in employment or a profession.

College Life—Finally Responsible for Self

One young man, like most of us in 1977, left home for the first time to university, a mostly unregulated environment where it was left to us to attend lectures if we liked, party all week if we so preferred, and put the necessary structure to our lives if we were to gain a degree in three or four years. For some inexplicable reason his preferred recreation was drinking. Within six months he was known as the fellow who shuffled around in a drunken daze day and night. He did not socialise much despite being at parties, and word soon went round that he did not attend lectures either. Luckily, this boy was from a well-known family of two doctor parents who were proactive, as he was soon whisked away for drying out before he was transferred to another university from whence he graduated well into a less eventful life.

Higher education is usually undertaken as a young adult new to the immense freedom that comes with leaving home and being free of adult monitoring for the first time. It is a time of life that should be fun and enjoyable, but the paradox is that attaining a good quality first degree or professional qualification during this time is the necessary foundation for the rest of your work life. You must therefore strive to find the right balance between fun and work to avoid a lifelong regret.

That first degree or qualification is a reference point for the rest of times, and it is amazing how the quality of a degree acquired forty years earlier is still mentioned when a 60-year-old is being cited!

The young person ought to take more than a fleeting interest in his or her own education. It is by assuming a participatory and responsible role in its development and direction that he or she would be diligent enough to make a success of it. Early engagement can be achieved through talks, parental interest and internships that could help establish genuine interest and commitment to the future.

At all stages of education, the guidance and involvement of parents, adults, and teachers cannot be overestimated. The adults in a young person's life at this stage of education must find the balance between not impeding while providing the necessary guidance that is required for success. The student, in most cases, might yet to attain full self-consciousness to make the right decisions without informed guidance.

Motivation in a child starts with the need to impress parents and teachers. This need to impress continues, albeit shielded, into young adulthood, and the adults in their lives should try to provide this motivation. It is only in very few and rare cases that a child becomes self-motivated from a very young age, which is why those few stand out. The adults should be attentive to any special needs (like the parents in the example) and possible hidden talents to ensure necessary support is provided.

Learning beyond the Classroom—Alternative Education

The good news for obtaining education is that many non-classroom options are increasingly available and continue to evolve, especially with the use of technology that has enhanced learning such that the Internet can take even the formal education stages beyond the physical classroom. Alternative forms of education designed for a general audience and their methods vary widely; they provide the opportunity for people who might have missed out on formal education to acquire useful education and skills for improving their quality of life. For adult students, a number of career and skill specific courses are available through the Internet in the form of self-directed learning. There is no shortage of opportunity to consciously take control of your own education at any stage of life despite a disadvantaged start.

Self-Development—Continuous Learning

The US Army's recruiting campaign used the slogan "Be All that You Can Be!" This is a call to not settle for mediocre, average, or anything less than what is possible; this can be described as a call to ensure potential is not wasted.

One of the greatest secrets of long-term success is personal development. Over time, we evolve and become someone new. The question is whether or not you intentionally grow to become the person you want to be. In the moments of life you can take steps to improve yourself, which is not as difficult as it may seem, or you may fizzle time away!

Personal development can be a delight once you get going and begin to see the results it yields. It is how you develop to live the on-purpose life you desire through the forging of your own self development plan. A plan that makes you constantly review your developmental needs and put in the effort to ensure that any knowledge gaps, which can change with your changing situations and goals, are addressed.

It has long been found that we all use only a small portion of our intellectual capacity such that only a fraction of our talent and ability is ever developed. We tend not to push ourselves to develop our potential because we are too busy or lazy or simply lack faith. If you study the ordinariness of the lives led by people who later became inventors, acclaimed artists, or software developers, you will find that self-development and dedicated effort played a pivotal role in their achievement. Apparently, Albert Einstein was not particularly brilliant at mathematics. He reportedly did not achieve top grades in school and could not get a teaching place when he graduated. He went on to publish his special theory of relativity while working as a clerk in the post office! He made the effort to develop himself and ultimately brought himself out of his ordinary post office job.

Malcolm Gladwell, in his book *Outliers: The Story of Success*, insists that genius actually has very little to do with intelligence; rather, he believes that what most people call genius is the result of unusual dedication and effort. He talks about the mathematicians, musicians, scientists, and business leaders who transformed our world not because they were unusual people just 'born that way' but because they put dedication and focus into pursuing their passions.

That opportunity is available to each of us. While they worked or raised a family, these 'geniuses' also pursued a dream, improved themselves, and kept at it until breakthrough. That is self-development.

'We can't help getting older. But getting better is a choice.'

—Anonymous

Would your career be richer if a particular training programme would make you better at your job? Would your opportunities expand if you learned new skills or a new language? Would your retirement be richer if you read more financial literature? Can you gain from a mastermind group? Bookshops are rich in self-help materials covering just about any topic or proficiency. The effort and dedication to do any of those results in personal development.

Unfortunately, the truth is that inertia, comfort, habits, and ordinary patterns of life conspire to keep us where we are. Even when people are frustrated at work or wish they had more money, or better education, the prevailing tendency is to keep moaning and do nothing about it until their ambition evaporates. There is no doubt that in reality, life can be busy with obligations and commitments, but you also have the responsibility to improve your lot and become more than you are. The question is whether you are conscious enough and willing to direct the learning for your improvement or not. The idea of a planned and intentional personal development might sound like what only over-ambitious people do, but beyond the compulsory schooling, it is mainly up to you to keep improving yourself over the rest of your life.

Even job-related trainings should not be taken for granted or left to your employer's interest to train you in the direction you would prefer. The employer's training objectives might not be in synergy with your desired direction, and you need to participate in planning for the required training to your goal. Very few people devise specific plans for their own personal development. It is not what people generally do, and that's a shame and a waste of potential.

Wisdom Bringing Primordial Attention to Life

'Wisdom is the principal thing; therefore get wisdom: and with all thy getting get understanding.'

—Proverbs 4:7

I am sure you can identify someone in your circle of friends or family that you adjudge wise. We all know such people who, even when not in full knowledge of what we seek their advice about, are still able to give us a wise view of things that help us better navigate the situation.

An aspect of self-development in a conscious life should be the achievement of wisdom. A life benefits from wisdom that is beyond school knowledge. The skill of knowing how to play the required hand in each situation is not a product of school curriculum. The deep knowing that is wisdom arises through the simple act of giving a situation or something your full attention to arrive at a wise decision. Attention is primordial intelligence from full consciousness, and if you constantly feed your subconscious with enriching material and exposure, it dissolves the barriers created by conceptual thought. This is why cleverness devoid of wisdom can be counterproductive – because it is confined by thoughts conditioned by past experiences, dogmas, and self-interests.

Wisdom is beyond the ego mind, and by giving your full attention to the moment regarding anything, you can experience an intelligence far greater than the egoist mind can muster. This can be learnt by becoming at ease with not trying to conclude or interpret from preconceived thoughts and past experience. It allows spontaneous right action from simply aligning with fundamental truths born of a nonjudgmental stance to a situation by calling upon your total knowledge. Wisdom comes with a conscious effort to diminish the ego and a desire to act according to fundamental truths in reaching the best conclusion concerning a thing or situation. As wisdom allows for intelligence that uses all the resources within you without preconceptions or biases, your level of past self-development and diverse knowledge will determine how wise you are.

Learning from Others—Mentors and Role Models

'A good example is someone who knows the way, goes the way, and shows the way.'

—Anonymous

Though your education is subconsciously enriched by what other people teach and impact you with even when it is not intentional, you can consciously learn from other people by choosing them as mentors and role models through observation and teachings. Observing other people's lives either as role models or mentors is a veritable learning resource that can be easily employed but which many rarely turn to unless it is part of a formal work-related policy. Skills, values, or knowledge that can help progress your education, career, and job opportunities should be sought from those around you who possess the same. People are usually willing to help teach others as long as it is made convenient for them when genuine interest and seriousness is perceived in the learner.

Role Models

The term role model generally means someone who serves as an example, whose behaviour is worthy of emulation by others. A person who is an example of the desirable values, attitudes, and behaviours associated with a role. A good father should be a role model for his sons. Role models can be persons who distinguish themselves in such a way that others admire and want to emulate, like the first female brain surgeon can be a role model for other women striving in that field.

The role model you ought to seek is one who possesses the qualities you would like to have and who inspires you to be your very best. A role model is different from a mentor. A role model can be a stranger, and the learning is based on your observations and emulations of their qualities, whilst a mentor develops a relationship with you in which he or she passes on values and knowledge.

The responsibility of choosing who you model yourself after is yours, and that choice is in turn dependent on the desired life and lifestyle you have defined as the life you aspire to. It is however important that you are able to identify any particular unsavoury values or behaviours of a role model that are not in sync with your own life goals to avoid following another's life blindly. You should be clear, for example, if the family life of a professional role model does not fit your plans of family living!

An attentive observation of most lives around you provide lessons, sometimes it's from their mistakes you learn how not to behave. Sometimes very unlikely subjects, like subordinates and younger people, can teach you life skills that you admire. I learnt afresh focus, commitment, and willingness to pursue goals from some very young subjects, one of them my own son. I watched these young people apply at a top university and was astounded and full of admiration as they worked vigorously at academics and extracurricular activities. I was immensely proud to see all in the group, without exception, gain admission to their chosen colleges. I have gleaned from my other son the benefit of patience and a non-judgmental stance in arriving at more robust decisions.

Mentors

Mentorship is a relationship in which a more experienced or knowledgeable person helps guide a less experienced one. This kind of arrangement is named from the Greek mythology Homer's *Odyssey*.

Mentor, a friend of Odysseus, was placed in charge of his son, Telemachus, and of his palace when he left for the Trojan War. Because of Mentor's role with Telemachus of encouragement and help in dealing with personal dilemmas, his name, *Mentor,* has been adopted in English as a term meaning someone who imparts wisdom to and shares knowledge with a less experienced colleague.

You can learn a great deal to help your progress by getting into a mentorship program relevant to your work, career, or professional development as a protégé or mentee. Useful mentoring is more than just answering occasional questions or providing ad hoc help. It should be an ongoing relationship of learning, dialogue, and challenge. Both mentor and mentee should establish learning points and results expected from the process if it is not to waste time on both sides. The focus of mentoring is to develop the whole person, so the techniques are diverse depending on the particular situation. I have taken on professional mentorships in the past just to find myself counselling mentees' spouses before long!

Mining Your Potential

If education is to have a formative effect on your mind, character, and physical ability, it becomes your responsibility to employ all available forms of education and learning to enrich and attain your consciously defined life and potential. You can only achieve much by learning much. Education, especially when self-directed, can be the critical success factor in achieving a great life. Your personal commitment to a lifelong mind-set of education and self-development will help you effectively mine your potential.

TO-DO
x 2
x 3
TIME
TEAM
EXELENT
TIME to WORK!
STRATEGY
PLAN:
Don't FORGET!
I ♥ my JOB
PAPERWORK

Chapter 4 – Work and Career

'Find out what you like doing best and get someone to pay you for doing it.'

—Katherine Whitehorn

What's the Point of Work?

The importance of work as a source of fulfilment, apart from providing a livelihood, is not understood by many. The observation of lives where there is no constructive work either because of unwillingness or lack of motivation resulting from sufficiency from an inheritance, shows how uninspired and listless the lack of work can make a life. We all complain about our work, sometimes just out of habit or a herd mentality but if you can imagine waking up everyday, apart from vacation time, without work to look forward to, that life would be meaningless. It would be a sure recipe for mental disorders like depression or the proverbial devil finding work for the idle hand! Work is necessary for a life to endeavour, to grow, to be productive, and to be fulfilled.

'No one who rises before dawn fails to make his family rich.'

—*A Chinese saying*

Beyond fulfilment and purpose financial reward is a very good motivation to work, especially as financial compensation is usually critical to achieving a planned lifestyle. Similar to many Chinese sayings connecting hard work to financial security, my native Yoruba have their own version of warning you off slacking. It translates thus:

"The one who waits for the inheritance lends himself to poverty".

Experience has proven this saying to be very true. The expectation of an inheritance and the resulting absence of motivation to earn a living tend to rob people of the inspiration to work. Such a person may never experience the fulfilment that comes with achievement, which in itself is a form of poverty. Furthermore, the ship of inheritance tends to come in a bit later in life and maybe not even as laden as expected – by when it is too late for the slack inheritor to mine his or her own potential and thereby tend to poverty.

The deeper ramification of this saying is that it is important to work even if an inheritance awaits one. The mind-set of a person that is concentrated on waiting for an inheritance is usually different from that needed to approach life with self-motivation and hunger for success through hard work. In the final analysis, the inheritor that lacks a work ethic and wealth-building experience would be more prone to losing the inheritance through carelessness or sheer ignorance, tending to poverty in the end. This is, of course, not a discouragement from building an inheritance or, for that matter, being inheritors; it is the reliance on inheritance as an excuse for not needing to engage in purposeful and fulfilling work that the saying warns against. If the inheritor were to have proper direction and motivation to find his or her life's work, within the estate or out of it, then the truism would not be applicable.

Work is purposeful effort, the physical or mental effort we direct to making or doing something of value. This discourse is about the importance of being conscious in determining the line of fulfilling work that you are best talented for and to excel at it. If your life's work would be purposeful and be of value, you ought to pay keen awareness to deciding and planning what that line of work would be. You also need to intentionally be the best you can be at it to find fulfilment in the long run.

A Most Important Decision

The choice of accountancy in my university application was principally made by my dad, bless him. To be fair though, he did a good job of convincing me of the profitable career opportunities in the finance industry. When I was accepted to study accountancy at university, I only thought as far as the graduation ceremony, and after that, during my professional studies, the pride of qualifying so young was my longest view. I was quickly recruited by a top accountancy firm at 24; at that point, I only recall having a hazy view of what the future held and being constantly stressed about timesheets and client responsibilities. I forged a career in accountancy and audit practice in the next ten years to good career progress. I then intentionally changed to banking ten years later, and after eight years in that line of work, I became a business owner.

Without underrating the dividends of career opportunities, experience, training, and livelihood of my first twenty years of work, which have continued to serve me to date, I believe it was at 45 that I finally came into a line of work that I consider the best fit for my aptitudes and talent. Managing a portfolio of investments mainly in real estate keeps me interested and fulfilled. I am lucky that I finally found that fit while I still had some work left in me. Many never do. The secret is to be diligent in seeking that fit even as you work at the available opportunities.

Your Career Choice and Decision

There are a few theories about career choice and development. They are generally based on developmental life stages, self-concept, and personality types. Self-realization take place mostly during adolescence and young adulthood and this is the period that thought is first given to the line of work to sign up to. Around the ages of 14 to 18 the adolescent starts to have ideas of work in relation to their self-concept and probably observation of role models. Then between the ages of 18 to 22 young adults narrow their career choices and begin focusing time and energy on attaining required education and skills for their choices. This is probably the most precarious stage, as a wrong choice of subjects of study can hamper for a long time if not for life.

By 24, education and training completed, it is time to hit the work force, and then the choice of type or aspect of work within their proficiency and training becomes of utmost importance. A lawyer might choose to work in a corporate set up rather than go into legal practice and the courts. From the age of 30 onward, usually the die being cast by now is when a careerist concentrates effort to climb the ladder of success within his or her chosen career. While these theories suggest how people generally choose a career, for many people this decision remains a long and fluid process. Choosing an occupation for life can be tricky especially as this happens at a relatively young age. It is rare to find an 18-year-old that is fully equipped to make that decision as occupational knowledge might not kick in until much later around the mid-twenties. Access to career guidance and counselling apart from internship opportunities is therefore invaluable at the tertiary education stage.

To choose a career that will make you happy, interested, and satisfied, you should start by assessing your skills, aptitudes and talent. Learn about the advantages and disadvantages of these possible choices and make wide enquiry of those experienced in your field of interest. A career choice can serve you all your life or become the choice you never really made.

Your Personal Fulfilment

Your recognition of the fundamental life's need for work beyond financial compensation should make your choice of work well considered. Personal fulfilment and contribution to society in whatever way your talent allows should be pivotal in this all-important decision. Apart from providing a livelihood and personal fulfilment, work also forms the basis for an inter-human framework to life beyond the family that serve life at many levels. Lifelong friendships are fomented at work that could not be available elsewhere. Beyond all these, significant training and experience in life skills such as teamwork, leadership, and tolerance are gained through work. You will find as life progresses that your society would be mostly created and supported by your line of work.

Your choice of fulfilling work from the different options, ranging from the most common employment and profession, to business building or the non-profit sector, should be based on your talents, skills, and temperament on the one hand and your financial and lifestyle goals on the other. Leaving the selection of your life work to chance is abdicating choice and responsibility. While you might take the advice and mentorship of others that have succeeded in your chosen line of work, the choice has to be ultimately yours. The clarity and consciousness that you bring to choosing your life work would help you cope with any challenges that might arise along work-life's path. You are more likely to be committed to dealing with such challenges and focussing on achieving your career and work goals if you chose the path consciously. For the same reason you are more likely to excel therein.

Subconsciously, choice of work is an area of life where cultural and societal affectations inadvertently come into play. Coming from a family line of professionals, or a race and culture where work ethics are defining will definitely affect an individual's choice of work but you must rank your personal fulfilment beyond all of these in your choice of work. Otherwise you could be headed for an early burnout or an unhappy work life of quiet desperation as many do. The choice and your intentionality should start with planning and choice at the education stage as pointed out in the preceding chapter. You should have intentionally chosen the appropriate degree to study that is beneficial for the work or career that suits you and will excite you.

Work Success... Diligence Is always Rewarded

'Success is based on imagination plus ambition and the will to work.'

—Thomas Edison

No matter the form of work you choose to dedicate yourself to – be it a business, a career in a profession, or a position in the non-for-profit space, you will find that the most critical factor for success remains diligence. There is evidence that there is a wide gap between the outcomes in cultures rooted in belief in the efficacy of their own meaningful hard work and those based on beliefs with expectations from providence and little correlation between their work and outcomes. The latter is typified by the Russian proverb. "If God does not bring it, the earth will not give it".

On the other hand, the Chinese have many sayings hugging success to effort. My favourites of these are: "If a man works hard, the land will not be lazy", and of course, "No one who rises before dawn fails to make his family rich".

Very little wonder that hard work is a familiar observation of the Asian culture and person. From school to university campuses to the workplace, the reputation of hard work sticks with the Asian. That cultural stereotype is definitely a success factor for that group. And it is worth emulating. Virtually every success story, if studied, involves someone working diligently and harder than their peers. Apparently, Bill Gates of Microsoft was addicted to his computer as a child, and so was Bill Joy, who wrote the JAVA computer language. The Beatles are reported to have put in thousands of hours of practice before they achieved renown.

The educational researcher Erling Boe stumbled by accident across a peculiar correlation between hard work and success. In administering a comprehensive maths and science test TIMSS (Trends in International Maths and Science Study) to students around the world, it was found that countries whose students take longer, are willing to concentrate, and are able to sit still long enough and focus on answering every question are the same countries whose students do the best at solving maths problems. It was found that these same countries that are best at solving maths problems appear to be those whose national cultures place high emphasis on effort and hard work. And guess which countries are top on the list? Singapore, South Korea, China, Hong Kong, and Japan. Cultures of diligence.

The study of the lives and circumstances of outliers shows that success definitely follow a predictable course. It is not the brightest who succeed. Outliers are ordinary people who have had the strength of character and presence of mind to seize their opportunities in a way that most people don't. That strength and presence of mind to seize opportunity, no matter your line of work, is diligence, and diligence is always rewarded.

Whatever the Work, the first Ten Years Are Critical for Success

The first ten years of work are pivotal. In counselling young people about work and life, I have come across a crop of 30 year olds who appear to have meandered for too long and seem lost, with only a hazy idea of where they are headed. They usually have hopped a few unrelated jobs or dabbled into different entrepreneurial endeavours after graduation. Finally, in realization that ten years have gone by, they seek counsel. It is very easy for this to occur when work is not consciously sought to build up a reasonable curriculum vitae (CV) in those critical years. A good starter job with a good employer focusses the mind of a young person while providing experience in work ethics and valuable training towards a good career. A pay packet also comes with a job, so you should not make a charity of yourself to parents, family, or friends as you wait endlessly for that elusive ideal job.

Whatever work you spend those first ten years doing must have concrete promise of value to a stakeholder (which could be yourself if planning to build a business) or the employment market in the future for it to be worth your time. If it is creativity, we must see the value in what you are doing – after all, Bill Gates abandoned college, but it was for a worthwhile and concrete purpose. A disjointed or nonexistent CV in the first ten years of what is expected to be your work life can have a long-term negative effect for finding work or being taken seriously thereafter. This should be avoided unless a curriculum vitae does not count to your future which could be so if you are dedicated to building your own business for example. Particular planning and effort should be made in this definitive period of your work life to make it a preparation and training for the service or career you intend to pursue.

Your Work Life Contour

What is termed the life contour of career or work is simply the path from starting one's work life up to retirement. The path of each career can be different because of personal circumstances, changes in interest, and external, uncontrollable factors. Ultimately, it is up to you to keep the life contour of your career in view and ensure appropriate changes are made as become necessary. To pay attention is to avoid a career in which you merely drift along without much progress or success.

Of course, most people enter the workforce with the hope of making a success of their choice, but you need to make adjustments upon entering an occupation by recognizing and developing the skills necessary to succeed in it. Over the years, staying employed and progressing your career, as simple as they may seem, require your attention and management. You either climb the ladder of success within your career, or you could get stuck somewhere in the middle! Failure to be conscious of the requirements for your career growth or to take responsibility for managing its progress can lead to a stunted career, despite your skills and brightness. Generally, a successful career is measured by acknowledgements through praise and in the form of promotion or a raise. Notice is success and usually there is an extreme drive for personal success among careerists because of this. Those who are ambitious and adept at playing the game end up gaining the notice and acknowledgements in an organization. As a careerist, you must determine a balance between commitment to career success and other important aspects of life like family and well-being to achieve the fulfilling life of balance that you seek.

The final stage of the career life contour is retirement, which, all things being normal, usually happens in later middle age. This stage need not create fright or anxiety if well considered and the transition planned long before it arrives. The feeling of shock, depression, or loss of identity and vibrancy that some experience at retirement is mostly due to a lack of planning. A warped work-life balance over the many years spent in a career can make careerists unprepared for life after or outside that career and can be bereft and lost when the social structure and trappings of work disappear suddenly. During a good career, it is imperative that life in retirement, no matter how distantly in the future it might seem, is carefully considered and planned to be equally fulfilling. This segment of life could span many years, and it can also be an enjoyable time of life if well organized ahead.

Work as a Business Owner

Working as a business owner can be by choice if you decide to build a business, or it could be thrust upon you through inheriting a family business, which can be a blessing if the business structures and systems are already in place (though they would need growing over time). No matter how you come to this line of work, you have to be passionate about your business and the product or service it provides in order to succeed in it. Building a business from scratch can be an exciting albeit risky endeavour. It takes passion and a lot of discipline and hard work to build or grow a successful business and to ensure its long-term survival. Just like the careerist gets training to excel in his work, you need to acquire relevant financial and industry skills and knowledge, especially at the earlier stages when the business cannot afford to engage all the required professional help.

Your financial goals for the business must be very clear to ensure value is being created. Too many times I see small business owners slave away with not much to show for it financially. Passion for a product or service is never enough reason to work in a business that needs to support your livelihood. The well-documented low probability of success of new businesses testifies to the fact that the burden of discipline, hard work, and dogma required at the building stage can be enormous and the journey lonely. Many people start businesses despite not having carried out enough research or gained understanding of the cash flow patterns of the particular business, and this is a recipe for failure. Gratification can be slow coming, but your focus must be the growth of the business. It is therefore critical that the owner of a budding business arms himself or herself, beyond interest and passion, with knowledge of practical matters like operating systems and finance relevant to the business chosen.

Some Matters Concerning Work to Be Mindful Of

There are aspects of the work life with far-reaching effects but which are not always treated with the importance they deserve. It is helpful if these issues are considered and approached in a proactive manner.

Work Ethics

Work ethic is a set of moral principles a person uses in their job. People who possess a strong work ethic embody certain principles that guide their work behaviour. Developing and exhibiting a strong work ethic will inevitably result in the production of high-quality work which will fuel the achievement of your goals. it is considered as a source of self-respect, satisfaction, and fulfilment.

Some factors that show good work ethic include being available, reliable, organised with the desire to do a task well.

On the other hand, A negative work ethic is behavior that would lead to a systematic lack of productivity and reliability with the resulting sphere of unhealthy relationships such as power politics and abuse of other workers.

Parents and guardians must help their young adults make the transition to mature adults fit for the work-place by ensuring they do not miss out on the discipline and self-discovery that work situations provide. Learning good work ethics has its rewards: it endows with self-sufficiency, confidence, and belief in one's own ability that all go to affect general self-esteem.

Work-Life Balance

The link between work and livelihood makes it an aspect of life that can be damaging if not consciously managed. Work and career, at least in a season, have a penchant for crowding out all else. For that reason and the extreme drive for personal success by careerists, work can decimate effective participation in other segments of life. Unfortunately, this anomaly is often realised too late when the harm is done and can scarcely be reversed. You must endeavour to find a balance between work and other also quite important areas and interests, like family, recreation, and well-being that bring balance to your life. It is helpful if you constantly ask yourself the question whether we work to live or live to work. I hope you know this is an equation because it must be balanced.

Misfit to Work and Lack of Fulfilment

Life can become pure drudgery when a person earns a livelihood from work that he or she is neither suited to nor talented for. Considering that work takes up to 70 per cent of our waking hours, misfit to work can mar the rest of life because of lack of fulfilment. If your work, say in employment, becomes totally unsatisfying, you ought to do all in your power to change jobs or line of work. Alternatively, you might be able to find some fulfilment beyond an unsatisfying work life by taking up an activity that interests you in your spare time. This would balance the feeling of drudgery from your day job and bring rewards beyond money in the form of self-realisation, sense of purpose, and joy.

Gender Issues

Without a doubt, cultural environment and biology contrive to have far-reaching implications for work in a woman's life despite the gains of modernity, feminism, and human rights advocacy. A woman who desires a career or full-time work would need to juggle work, family life, and sometimes motherhood. This reality should be well considered and planned for at the point of work-choice decisions. While the reality is that 'something' tends to give at some point in a mother's work life, you can still enjoy a balanced and fulfilling life if work decisions are made with clear objectives with the support of family. Luckily, the options of part-time work or exchanging a stressful work situation, say from being a doctor on ninety-six-hour call duties, for a more structured and conducive one are available and the workplace is increasingly supportive of motherhood.

End of Active Work Life

There are challenges associated with the end of the active work life that might not have been envisaged and planned for. These relate mostly to loss of perquisites or privileges and reduction in income at retirement. Also, the social network and human contact that come with work can suddenly fall away, leaving one bereft. Deep emotional depression and even illness can result if not well managed. Planning a post-retirement life and activities should be paramount towards the end of one's work life to make retirement the enjoyable rest and time of freedom it is supposed to be.

Your retirement plan ought to include a constant review of your finances in the five years preceding retirement, upon which you can easily move from an earning and accumulation mode to one of spending and management of accumulated capital. It takes some strategy for that not to cause anxiety and a reversal in lifestyle. As you plan your retirement, you need to work out an estimate of your monthly outlay to determine the income stream that would be needed and to put the appropriate earning assets in place sometime before the retirement parties and the gold wristwatch

To keep life vibrant, I hope you also find time to plan for post-retirement endeavour that would give you pleasure and keep you present in society. That is important so the rest of your life can be as satisfying as your working years.

DEBT
STOCKS
Savings
FINANCE
investment
income
tax
Financial Plan
Deduction
TAX
Bills
$$$
Planning

Chapter 5 – Financial Planning and Wealth Creation

It might be true that money cannot buy happiness but the fact that having enough of it affects so many aspects of life makes it a critical part of a consciously lived life. Simply put, money Answereth Too Many Things! It is therefore useful that a person who seeks to be effective in other aspects of life be prepared for the financial realities of modern-day life. Whether you are only responsible for yourself or take financial decisions for a whole family, learning how to manage money is an aspect of personal development that everyone needs and does not require gaining an accounting degree. All that is needed is enough knowledge to competently manage your affairs and know when and from whence to seek help as necessary.

I have been privy to the finances of two professionals in the last ten years, one a personal finance client of my practice, the other an acquaintance who bounces ideas off me regarding finance now and again but especially when she experiences cash flow problems.

The first, Rick was a middle level manager at one of the oil and gas majors when I was invited to talk to the company's managers about managing personal finance. He signed up for six-monthly advice and reviews, and we put together the building blocks of what his portfolio consists of today. We started by ascertaining his financial position and then determined the lifestyle to be funded over the years and their timeliness. We planned especially for when his two young children would be due for fee-paying education and what quantum and currencies that would be required for them. We have, in the past ten years, planned a mix of investments that would fit his desired lifestyle. Subsequently, his two children have since attended top schools , thanks to their education endowment. The family lives in their own property, and his career thriving. While his wife is not signed up under this arrangement, her financial participation in the family finance registers in the biannual reviews, and their net worth growth, which has been tracked, surpasses the usual indices.

The other, a young lady, Roslyn, had been very lucky with her career and grew to very senior positions fairly quickly as she moved from one good employer to another, usually with promotions. She would call me to ask for advice, but usually not when she made investments or planned them. It was usually to inquire how she could borrow as stop-gaps out of the banking system, and I was intrigued at these cash-flow strains because I knew she earned good salaries. On the other hand, she lived very flamboyantly: the cars, jewellery, clothes, and elite addresses stood out. She moved homes quickly, first from one rental property to another but finally to a home in a very smart and expensive part of town.

Then suddenly, she no longer had a job, and the need for the expensive short-term loans became desperate. Ultimately, she was found to be leveraged beyond an imaginable level. The sad truth is this lady never had a financial plan; she spent her salaries, leaving no surplus to save or invest. In terms of her lifestyle, she punched way beyond her weight with cars, jewellery, and other luxuries. She enrolled her children in schools she could not afford or ever planned for. She also lived in a mortgaged home that she could not afford. In the end she lost her home and was indebted to many lenders, including friends and family. She simply punched out of her league and lost it all. The big risk of losing it all at middle age is that it might be impossible to recover or regroup, and it is likely to be a fast downhill journey.

Managing Your Finances

So it is understandable that you will be busy, either with your career or business, and hardly able to fit your activities into the waking hours. Meanwhile, you are aware of the need to prioritize planning your future and finances, but you keep procrastinating. The misleading general belief that only the already wealthy need planning or management of their finance is a stumbling block for many. The reality is that the earlier the planning and management process starts, the better to take advantage of early opportunities and gain from the power of compound interest over time.

The first breakthrough for an individual in actively managing his or her finance is to take personal responsibility. An early understanding that the ultimate responsibility for managing and growing your net worth is yours will ensure your view of your finances is not limited to what your employer is willing to pay you or the gifts and inheritance from wealthy parents. Taking personal responsibility allows you to develop some vision of financial goals both for the short and long term. Each person's definition of enough money (that which ensures a financial peace of mind) depends solely on the desired and fulfilling lifestyle of the individual. While one person's financial paradise might be what is required to raise and educate the children, own a country home, and earn a fair amount of income in retirement; another person might seek a lifestyle that allows him or her extensive travel in retirement and a vacation home in another country. Financial goals are ultimately quantified statements of a desired lifestyle! It is a matter of different strokes for different folks.

To gain awareness and understanding in managing money early in life is to have a better chance at arriving at key stages with the confidence and control that financial independence brings. The writer Jim Rohn, in his teachings about money, would pose a question he learned to ask early in his career: Have you found the opportunity that is going to take care of you and your family for the rest of your lives?

Financial independence and success are down to finding and optimising these opportunities. Finding and harnessing those opportunities is a critical first step in the achievement of many lifestyle goals. Beyond finding opportunities, financial success is also about acquiring and reinforcing good money habits, because successfully managing personal finance results more from habit than technical knowledge. It is either a habit of discipline producing a cycle of mining opportunities, saving and investing for growth and income or one of reckless spending, spiralling debt with its prohibitive interest costs, and then some more borrowing. Usually a habit is formed by each cycle, which then becomes difficult to break the longer the habit is allowed to settle.

The time to start is right from the first pay packet when most life decisions are still ahead. If you have not started, no matter what stage of life you are, the best time is now! Planning and intentionally following the plan can only improve the situation.

Planning Your Finance for Success

The earlier you start paying attention to your finances, the longer the planning and implementation time you have to reach your goals. An early start definitely serves as a protection against being easily lured into high risk 'quick money deals' later in life in an attempt to attain financial objectives in a hurry. The general misconception that you can wait until later in life to start cannot be further from the truth, especially if you consider the number of early life decisions like career choice and family size that have long-lasting financial implications. You would have little room to manoeuvre when you already have four children in an average one-income family.

Planning and taking actions to achieve the plan is critical to financial success. Even those who inherit money need to plan how to sustain and grow to avoid losing what has been passed to them. The clear definition of what one seeks to achieve is essential to success. When money objectives are not very clear, it becomes easy to get distracted by other people's lifestyle and get derailed into striving to be like the Joneses and taking money decisions often based on social or cultural sentiments to one's ultimate regret.

How Soon?

As soon as you're able, as a young adult, to earn income and are in control of how it is spent, it is important that you begin to consider the levels to which you need to grow your net worth and income to support your desired lifestyle regarding family life costs that come with marriage and young children. You will find that it does not get cheaper as you move on to middle age, which arrives sooner than you expect. Then old age, which could be a very long spell with the ever-improving mortality due to medical technology and healthier lifestyle, can be a time of anguish if not well planned. If net worth and income have not been grown to replace the loss of earned income at retirement, the old age costs of regular medicals, travels and continued participation in society can stack up very high.

Financial planning is beyond periodically putting some money away and acquiring assets in a haphazard manner. You need to set net worth destinations, timelines, deadlines, and a roadmap of the route most suited to achieving your goals to ensure that such savings and assets are well directed. A good plan will help ensure they are appropriate in terms of timing, location, and maybe currency. Investments intended to fund children's education, for example, have to be timed to mature when the fees would be due and currency-hedged for the location of the schools. The differences in each person's current financial position, age, personal circumstances, and the financial implications of lifestyle goals makes it imperative that each person's financial plan is customized.

The help of a good financial planner (not the ones who also sell investments and legal products as they could be conflicted) can be invaluable for people who are too busy with their jobs or other businesses to pay adequate attention to developing and monitoring a financial plan. An independent financial adviser's basis for recommending investment products for clients would be unbiased and directed to optimising yields and risks to meet each client's financial objectives. They are usually in a better position to advise timely modification to plans where necessary because of their access to information and research. Planning is the bridge between now and your lifestyle goals; to ensure the achievement of those goals, you require a plan of how to get there!

Your Current Status Is Where to Start

Any planning process can only start with a clear view of the current status. Therefore, the preparation of your current net worth statement, coupled with the analysis of your sources of income, expenses, and obligations, is the natural starting point for a financial plan. It is also quite simple.

<u>Computing Your Net Worth Statement</u>

Assets: It is not difficult to prepare a comprehensive list of *all* your assets that can realize some monetary value if the need arises. This would include but not limited to real estate, cars, money in bank accounts, and holdings in companies and businesses. As long as you have an idea of the present open market value of each item, it should be included in the computation. It is important that you know that there is a clear difference between assets and luxuries. For this purpose, only belongings that can be exchanged for value or investments able to achieve capital appreciation or yield, are considered assets. Otherwise, they are luxuries. That jetty built in attachment to your rented home, the sports car, or the Hermes bag are all luxuries, not assets. Luxury goods like cars, non-tradable jewellery, and clothes (unless they have vintage value) would have considerably lower value than their cost once they have been owned.

Liabilities: Now prepare a list of all your loan obligations, including mortgages, cars, and other asset loans. Amounts owed to others, including family and friends, are not exempted. The fact that the market value of the assets on which such liabilities were incurred might have reduced does not diminish your obligation. This should be particularly borne in mind in the case of reduced prices due to the volatility of the capital market.

Once you have computed both lists, deduct the total liabilities figure from the total assets and you have your net worth. If your net worth is positive with assets and investments greater than liabilities, then *congratulations* are in order: you are part of a minority with a positive net worth. If the result is negative, that is not necessarily bad news. It is how the liabilities have been put to use that is important; they could result in capital appreciation in the future if assets have been invested in. Even if the negative net worth has not resulted from valuable assets, it is useful that you now know the size of the hole to fill before you can grow a positive net worth.

<u>Computing Your Net Income Statement</u>

Just as important as your net worth is your net income. This is because apart from capital appreciation on assets, net income is another contributor to the growth of your positive net worth.

Income: A comprehensive list of *all* your income from wages, bonuses, rentals, interests or dividends, and other contracted inflow from other sources.

Expenses: These are *all* your expenses, including rent, interest payable on mortgages and other loans, utility bills, groceries, fuel, and even expenses as irregular as expenditure on dining out should be included in order to get a true picture.

Deduct total expenditure from total income to obtain your net income. If you are disciplined, you should have a positive figure, which would be available to put aside as savings or for investing. The computation of your net income as a monthly figure can be misleading as there could be some income and indeed expenses prepaid or owed on an annual or quarterly basis; you would need to include the monthly equivalent of these in the statement to ensure your net monthly income figure is accurate.

<u>What Does Your Current Status Show?</u>

Both your net income and net worth should have positive figures. The higher the positive figures, the better your financial health. A positive net income suggests you're living within your means and have attained a level of financial independence, while a positive net worth signifies a sound financial health that would allow wealth creation if you put your mind to it.

It is common in young adulthood to have a positive net income or barely break even while your net worth remains negative because of liabilities on assets you have acquired through mortgages or long-term loans. For this reason a positive net income could give a distorted view of your financial stature for the simple reason that it only confirms living within your current means. It would include only the interest cost of loans as expenses but would not consider the future repayment of those liabilities. It is therefore important to understand and keep in mind that a positive net income or cash flow does not necessarily signify financial soundness and should be considered in conjunction with the net worth to obtain a better measure of your financial status. In leveraged situations, where borrowing is for valuable and tradeable assets, the inclusion of the value of the assets to which borrowings have been applied would affect the net worth either positively or otherwise.

If you are at a negative net income or net worth or indeed both, all hope is not lost. This exercise should have shown you the importance of taking immediate steps to develop a plan to remedy the situation and avoid deterioration! The objective should be to achieve both positive net income and net worth and then grow them in order to create some wealth.

Setting Your Financial Goals and Achieving Them

Setting goals and developing the plans to achieve them becomes the logical next step once the reality of your current financial position is established. That current status becomes the destination from whence you wish to depart, while setting goals is like defining the place you would rather be. Most people have a vague idea of their desired lifestyle but only a few take the time and make the effort to define the contents and features thereof. In defining this new destination, lifestyle goals encompassing living standards, recreational needs, the planned quality of education for children, what you intend to do in retirement, even your charity interests become the building blocks. As these become your set goals, their financial implications have to be quantified to ascertain the required levels of income, assets, and investments that would support these lifestyle goals. These are your financial goals to which you have to commit and find the path.

Armed with self-knowledge and realistic consideration of your line of work, a strategy and plan of actions can be developed. A long-term plan is better broken down into medium-term subsets for clarity and manageability. A medium-term view is usually clearer and easier to manage as socioeconomic conditions change over time. I find that the use of intermediate destinations, roadmaps, and deadlines help avoiding distractions while grappling with daily living. Goals, both long-term and shorter-term, are the destinations while required actions and tactics to achieve them constitute your roadmaps. Realistic time deadlines fixed for arriving at each destination would also propel you to attain those goals. Even when deadlines are sometimes missed, the proximity to your destination means you are likely to make the extra effort to cross the finish line and if not, you would end up in close proximity of your goal.

Close monitoring of your financial plans is a sure way to their achievement. In money matters, only what is monitored and measured will materialise. It is by constantly evaluating your achievements against set goals that you will ensure there is no derailment from the plan and take necessary steps for any amendments or redirection that might be needed. If such evaluations are difficult for you because you lack financial skills or are simply too busy at your day job, I recommend that you enlist the services of a financial adviser.

Over time, changes in circumstances and forecasts can make it necessary to amend plans, and it is only by keeping your eyes on the ball that you avoid nasty financial surprises further down the road. Changing interest regimes or regulations that could affect values in your plan can be timely addressed before any harm is done. The process of monitoring and appraising would make apparent such needed amendments to plans and sometimes the roadmap in accordance with changing circumstances and information. Recognition of achievements during these periodical reviews will motivate further to delay gratification and maintain discipline for value adding activities. You can improve the whole planning and monitoring process by seeking professional help if you are unable to be effective in this exercise because you cannot make time or do not have the know-how.

Wealth Creation Principles

There are timeless general principles for managing finance and growing wealth. These have remained the same from Babylonian days to date and will not fundamentally change although their applicability might be different for each person, circumstances, or economic conditions. If you observe the life of those who have had to make and grow some wealth, you would see the evidence of the application of these principles with the attendant success in their situations.

Wealth Mind-Set

One of the key concepts to creating wealth is to understand that obtaining a certain amount of money in itself, say a million dollars, cannot be the goal. Frequently, people say they want to be wealthy, but what they are really after are the things money can buy and the freedom to do whatever they want. While you may think this is not significantly different from being wealthy, it is actually the reason so many people never become wealthy. This is because the money habits that create wealth are very different from those that serve instant gratification. The ability to spend uncontrollably is never the goal of someone with a wealth mind-set.

Another hindrance is that most of us were taught throughout our childhood that the whole point of making money is to sock it away and build our own nest egg. We think of this as a type of insurance against bad fortune, or old age when we can no longer work. The wealthy know that money only works when it is in motion, not when it has been left just sitting in a bank account. You must understand that wealth is an ongoing journey of growth and circulation, and if that circulation is stopped, value begins to reduce.

While it may seem that there are many roadblocks on the journey to wealth, the only real obstacle is what you believe, think, do, and feel about money. You might have heard the cliché "Seeing is believing", which is a sceptical view of life. Still, having heard it your whole life, it could become part of your thought process and mind-set without your being conscious of it. The wealthy understand that this cliché is actually backwards for wealth creation; you must believe in your vision of what you want to achieve and act on that belief before you can see it happen in real life. They know that "Believing and acting is seeing". The only thing that separates a millionaire from the have-nots is a wealth mind-set, and the foundation of that mind-set is belief in a vision and working to make it happen.

Does this mean the wealthy have some special skills or knowledge? No, but they do possess some key characteristics that help them become wealthy. The first of these characteristics is a willingness to listen to their own heart, which can make the journey somewhat lonely. If you could become wealthy by listening to the masses, then the masses would be wealthy, but they are not. It is a natural tendency to ask the opinions of those we love or respect, but unfortunately, listening to their comments and biases, and not taking into account the results of those biases in their own lives can be limiting. We frequently make a decision to listen based on emotional attachment rather than by looking at the empirical data of what such advisers are likely to know. How can anyone who has not accumulated wealth advise you on how to do it? They likely can't. You should listen to your heart and take advice from those who would know.

A second characteristic of the wealth mind-set is the ability to perceive and act when opportunities present themselves. Opportunity is often imagined to be something glaring that you cannot miss or pass up. However, opportunity is often only a gentle impression that comes during some of the most unclear or hazy times of life. If you read the stories of very wealthy and successful people, you will frequently find they were fired from jobs, rusticated or expelled from college, or were dealt some significant personal problems that other people would view as devastating. Instead, they take the challenges as opportunities and prosper.

A success factor that surprises and maybe annoys many people is that the wealthy are never wasteful. They understand that wealth is an ongoing process and is a result of careful management of resources. Also, they know it is rarely accomplished overnight, although it can sometimes occur in a short period of time. When wealth comes in a sudden bang, it can only endure if the person has prepared and been prepared over time and already possesses a wealth mind-set. Those who gain wealth before they have gained a wealth mind-set, say in the case of a lottery win, are in danger of losing that money because of waste. This is why we often hear of people becoming penniless a few years later because they never learnt to think wealthy and ultimately fritter away whatever money they get by chance.

Whether you grow up in the worst circumstance or have every advantage, you can develop a wealth mind-set. However, no matter how much you dream about becoming wealthy, it is not likely to happen until you put that mind-set and its attending habits into action.

Know Your Path

Self-knowledge is critical in deciding the route through which you intend to build wealth. You are most likely to succeed by doing what you are inspired to do and know best to do. If serious and thoughtful consideration is given to John Rhon's advice regarding finding that opportunity that is going to take care of you and your family for the rest of your life, your work or career decision could be that opportunity that becomes your path to financial freedom and wealth. Once you have recognised the route(s) that are best for you to take, you must take steps to train yourself to become knowledgeable and effective in making the appropriate financial decisions .

In this matter, recognition needs to precede action because oftentimes people dabble without considering what they would be most productive and fruitful in doing. A major stumbling block to financial success in many lives results from covetously or erroneously seeking to replicate the path of other people who have been successful. The truth is we each possess different and particular combinations of skills and temperance that makes each able to excel in what we are best at. It easier to make your own luck and find opportunities when you're in your most fulfilling endeavours that you're most talented for.

You'll observe that the successful do what they believe in, and they make money at it. Wealth usually follows as a logical result. In reality, wealth exists within each of us if we find and do something we are naturally inspired to do and love.

A successful lawyer friend said something profound as we discussed some investments. He said over the more than thirty years since graduation from college, he has found that the only work he has had financial success in without undue stress or failure is in the practice of law, and it was not for want of trying other lines of business. Of course, he is able to invest in assets outside his law practice, but his potential for greatness is in the practice of law.

Self-knowledge includes being aware and conscious of your money attributes (you could be a spender, a saver, or even a hoarder) and constantly manage and consider these in planning towards achieving your financial objectives. Be sincere in acknowledging such attributes to enable you better manage any weaknesses, harness your strengths, and work on acquiring required skills and habits for your particular route.

Draw Your Purse Strings—Saving as Much as Possible

Living within one's means is a challenge to the employee as it is to the successful businessperson. While earning more money is usually most people's focus, another approach to growing net worth is actually by the way of the good old saving: not wasting money and saving a good portion of what you already earn. Many people keep excess funds in various deposit accounts, but this is not advisable. Your savings should be planned ahead and to specific timelines and purposes. The risk in unplanned savings is that it is not very different from keeping cash at home. They are usually viewed as emergency funds for a rainy day, and those tend to come fast and often. When there is a financial need, even when not so urgent, there is always the temptation to deplete such savings. Also, as is common, when saving is not deliberate, the interest earned might be much lower than the current inflation rate, which is a loss in effective value.

Some discipline is all it takes to save ... but it is easier to be disciplined when saving occurs as part of planning towards a goal.

A good strategy to grow savings is to *pay yourself first* – by ensuring a defined percentage of your income is the first deduction towards your savings or investments, after the contractual obligations like rent but before other lifestyle expenses, regardless of how much your income is. The idea is borne out of treating all your outflows that are not obligatory as paying or meeting the financial needs of the different recipients. Your clothes and accessory shopping bill pays the shop-owner, and your expensive dining and vacation costs help keep the restaurateur and holiday company in business. If you do not pay yourself first, you literarily work to pay and satisfy the financial needs of other stakeholders, each interested in getting some of your pay packet. Be conscious that you happen to be one of those stakeholders, so endeavour to pay yourself first by saving towards investing for future income and value appreciation.

Probably worse than lacking the discipline to save is the use of borrowed money for conspicuous consumption with the attendant cost of borrowing. Never underestimate the power of compound interest for increasing your savings or exploding your borrowings!

Delaying gratification can be a challenge in particular to very well-paid professionals. Substantial salaries can be mistakenly treated as income available for acquiring luxuries and living an unsustainable lifestyle of expensive habits. In the real sense, a good proportion of such salaries should be saved towards assets that would provide future income and lifestyle. Luxuries should only be bought with income derived from assets or investments, which is the real proof of affordability.

A saving habit should lead first to building an emergency fund and then to further savings. Ideally, you should have an emergency fund with a minimum of a few months' wages in a liquid investment for any financial surprises. The emergency fund acts as a buffer, which should replace the use of credit cards and other borrowings for emergency situations. The size of an emergency fund depends on the particular circumstances and possible emergencies. For someone who lives in a rented home and has only a modest amount of debt, an emergency fund of $1,000 may work fine. However, if you own a house, a car, and have a family, increasing the possibility of unexpected needs for cash infusion, then your emergency fund will need to be larger. The strategy is to build the fund by consistently devoting a certain percentage of each paycheque towards it and ensure that the fund is only used for true emergencies.

What is an emergency? An unplanned holiday with friends over a long holiday weekend at an expensive location is not an emergency. When your main or only car suddenly breaks down and an expensive part needs repair, or your water heater starts to hiss and spit green bile, then you have an emergency. Covering regular purchases like clothes, food, and wine do not count. With an emergency fund in place, you should soon eliminate the use of credit card debt at great cost when life throws you a financial surprise.

Multiple Streams of Income

Whether you are in employment or building a business, creating multiple streams of income is essential. Part of your long-term financial planning process should be to avoid dependence on one source – for example, one salary in a household. Alternative streams will help wean you off dependence on just one income. The additional income could be as simple as the salary of a spouse or investment income from another activity.

As much as we hope not, contingencies and unplanned loss of income do happen. Job security is increasingly not guaranteed, and jobs are now rarely assured until retirement. Premature retirement and permanent disability do occur. Notwithstanding the availability of an insurance cover, the shock resulting from the suddenness in change of status, as well as the time it could take to refocus or get re-employed could lead to desperation in a one-income-dependent situation.

In creating alternative income streams, decision and choice should be based on careful analysis of how productive an alternative source would be without constituting a distraction from your core activity. Also, care should be taken for it not to become a financial drain rather than another stream of income. While capital market investment is a usual choice and can be a veritable source of income and capital gain, if not well managed, it could result in losses or constitute a stagnant pool of funds at best. To ensure that you get the most from your other sources of income, they should be dedicated to building up savings and investments or an emergency fund. Increasing your income without a planned use to mop up the extra income tends to result in the gains being squandered.

Continually Seek Opportunities to Increase Value through Profitable Ventures

Having set financial goals, it remains your job to constantly seek good opportunities to achieve them. One advantage of set goals is that it encourages you to be on the lookout for opportunities. In seeking such opportunities, however, their profitability or potential value must be well assessed before they are embarked upon. The potential for value appreciation or income generation should be present for them to be adjudged good opportunities. The need to research and understand the dynamics of ventures is critical; it is common to see people invest in ventures they do not properly understand or that in fact do not fit into their investment profile just because the opportunity was suggested to them by someone.

Do seek professional advice about an investment or venture to better equip you in making a decision if you are not knowledgeable about it. While it would be a shame to keep missing out on opportunities for lack of knowledge or fear of the unknown, you should be confident enough to say no when necessary. If you do not understand a venture or your questions have not been adequately addressed and you have an uncomfortable feeling about the transaction or the parties involved, you should decline. Other opportunities would come by. Ultimately, the ability to make and grow money is a combination of your preparedness and opportunities. The extent of your preparation helps you to recognize good opportunities when they present themselves. Ensure your preparedness by acquiring as much knowledge as possible as pertains to your area of endeavour, and keep focus on the set goals.

Dealing with Bad Money Habits

Everyone should carry out an unflinching reality check to identify and acknowledge bad money habits that might stand between them and financial success. Many people believe that purchasing power and its gratification is the measure of financial success. The spending impulse is natural, but the key to success is learning not to make a habit of giving in to that primal urge, especially when you cannot afford it (and recognizing that you truly cannot afford it).

The fact that you have the liquidity (sometimes in the form of a credit card) for a purchase does not mean you can afford it. As long as important obligations such as children's education or payment of outstanding debts suffer as a result of that immediate and unnecessary spending, you really cannot afford it.

The meaning of affordability is often misunderstood. Affordability is relative. It is not derogatory but merely a statement of limit or even priority. It is a matter of priority if, for example, you consider a holiday unaffordable only because of a preference to plough the available funds into a more profitable venture or to reduce borrowing to a reasonable level.

The most dangerous money habits that are also difficult to break are those formed from childhood. Children observe family and society in which they are nurtured; bad habits can be formed from hearing money discussions that make lasting impacts and subconsciously build a wrong belief system and attitude about money. If you grew up in a home where profligacy and general lack of discipline were the norm, chances are you would have the wrong concept of money. It will take a very conscious effort on your part to change those values. If, on the other hand, you grew up under frugal conditions, you are likely to have incubated some good habits and be disciplined in handling money.

Personal traits and temperaments could also affect spending habits. Addictive and obsessive dispositions, for example, could be the underlying factors for money affectations in people. The most frequently exhibited money habits include overspending (living beyond your means), abdication of responsibility (not taking necessary action), and holding an unrealistic view due to a lack of knowledge – and yes, stinginess and fearfulness in spending can be bad money habits too! The healthiest money attribute to instil is to make an effort to live within your means no matter how small those means are! If you are disciplined for long enough, a habit will be formed that becomes the path to financial success.

Differentiating between Leverage and Borrowing for Consumption

An area that is generally shrouded in both confusion and ignorance is the management of debts. Dealing with bank loans and other unpaid bills may seem boring or scary to the point of not wanting to deal with them; however, ignoring them will not make them go away. Committing to taking charge of your finances is maturity and empowerment. Paying attention to this area of your finance can be sobering and would curb impulse spending and taking on of unnecessary loans in the future. For the self-employed, the usual error is that of confusing personal cash flow and borrowings with those of their business. The temptation is to mortgage the family home for funding the business, it is common to find that the failure of the business is quickly followed by the failure of their family life because of the leverage connection between the two.

Borrowing, of course, can be a necessary and sound tool to provide leverage for an opportunity that involves a substantial capital outlay like mortgages for real estate investments. You should be clear that the expected returns on the investment (ROI) outweigh the interest and other charges payable on the loan. The timing of the expected exit or liquidity events from such investments should also be planned to be aligned with the tenor and repayment covenants of the related loans. Failure to carefully do this can result in loss of expected profits or even loan failure such that the asset value is not enough to allow you walk free.

Unless it makes financial sense to do so, you should try to avoid debt as far as possible as it can lead to a depletion of both your net income and net worth. Remember, the loan itself is a liability, which reduces your net worth whilst interest charges reduce your net income by increasing your expenses. Borrowing for recurring living expenses or unaffordable luxury should be avoided by all means. A very slippery pitfall is debt under the guise of bargains at sales and special discounts funded by credit. It is good to remember that a bargain is not a bargain unless you need the item in the first place and you can afford the discounted price without resorting to credit.

Principles of Investing

Investing and managing your investment portfolio can be one of the most financially rewarding activities, but it can also be quite unnerving. So much of investing is tied to personal aspirations, inhibitions, and fears that it can be difficult separating the real from imagined risks. The fact that the world of investing can itself be overwhelming prevents many people from participating. However, investing, in one form or another, would be necessary to achieve growth in net worth. This is true even when your financial opportunity is in a highly rewarding career, and at some point, a pension investment pot has to be created to keep you in the lifestyle you are accustomed to when you retirement.

Deciding What to Do with Money

The moment value is received, you immediately have a choice to make: to either spend it or invest it. Investing is to trust others to borrow it or use it to create value on your behalf if you are not a business owner. Your choice of what to do with that value should indicate your intentions and the outcome you seek. Spending it provides immediate gratification. If you decide to store it in cash equivalents, it provides liquidity and availability for you to use at any time, though inflation is likely to be eroding its buying power over time. If you want to put your value to work in one of many possible investment vehicles, you would need some investment strategy to guide you in doing so. Whichever investment vehicle you may choose, investing means parting with your value in the hope that what it has been exchanged for will increase your net worth through income and or value appreciation.

There are basic strategies governing investing, and being a successful investor means finding the right strategy that suits your circumstances and meet your goals while optimising your risk-reward balance of investing.

Investment Strategies

Although each of the investment strategies is geared towards particular investment objectives, most investors would need to combine strategies to meet their particular circumstances and objectives.

Capital Protection

A capital protection strategy would seek to safeguard value already built up in a portfolio. Safety is the top priority here but that does not translate to a do-nothing stance. Doing nothing with money allows inflation to erode its buying power and thereby diminish its value over time. For protection, an investor must keep close control by lending for short periods of time, to reliable borrowers like governments or invest in assets or businesses of reputable track record. Such borrowers, because of their credit rating or the short tenor of the investment which limits the use to which they can put the funds, would only pay a marginal interest or coupon for such limited use of funds. That is an acceptable trade-off for an investor who needs to protect value from the effect of inflation and loss to riskier investments. However, lending for even short periods can expose an investor to some risks which is why the reputation of who it is lent to is critical. A good vehicle for protection is short-term deposits with reputable institutions or government bills.

Earning Income

The investment objective and priority here is earning of regular income that will outpace inflation to provide real returns. An income stream strategy is for the investor that needs to receive regular instalments of income with some predictability in amount and timing. Funds are invested for longer periods to allow the borrower time and stability to produce a predictable stream of income. You would in return expect to be better compensated for taking the added risk that is a by-product of parting with money for a longer period. The most common examples of lending for earning regular income are corporate and government bonds.

Growing Value

A growth strategy for investing is aimed at achieving increase or appreciation in value, as much, as fast and as safely as possible. A growth strategy requires investors to give up the most control with a significantly lower level of predictability about the success of projects in which they are invested. In return for unpredictability and loss of control, growth investors expect to be better compensated than protection and income stream investors within a reasonable time period. If the compensation, usually in the form of capital appreciation, does not materialise, this could mean taking a loss on an investment. The risk-return payoff must be firmly kept in view and managed in a growth portfolio to avoid disproportionate losses.

Combining Strategies

There is usually a need to combine strategies as most investors would have a combination of investment needs. Some of your money might need absolute protection for use at a specific time for a purpose while the balance can be available for growth over a longer period. You may also need some regular income for recurrent living expenses. Some investments are designed to meet two or more investment purposes.

For example, some equity investment funds are designed to generate income, achieve growth, and provide liquidity if they are freely traded. An investor may be willing to sacrifice some of the potential of one strategy in exchange for meeting dual requirements. If the intention is to meet many investment objectives in one portfolio, it is important that you understand and employ asset allocation principles to appropriately diversify your portfolio asset classes and the attendant risks.

Watching Those Investment Risks!

There are risks inherent in investing that would affect the result or outcome of your investments. These must be borne in mind and be constantly managed to optimize value and returns from your portfolio. How you approach risk and the types of risk you are willing to take on depends on your risk appetite. While your risk appetite is mostly a reflection of your temperament, it should also be dictated by the state of your finance and stage of your life. It is advisable that risk appetite be tempered with advancing age, because the chance of recovery from significant losses reduces in later life. The level of knowledge and information you possess to carry out such assessment can further affect your appetite in taking risks because knowledge gives confidence in approaching and managing risk. Finally, the risk-reward trade-off should always be well considered as potentially high returns on risky investments can be very tempting. The general rule is that high rewards tend to bear higher risks, and only investors who are competent to manage those levels of risk should venture therein. The usual risks that need consideration in acquiring and managing investments have to do with the investment decision itself, those inherent in changes in interest and exchange rates and of course inflation. There are also unforeseeable risks depending on the location of the investment in the form of sovereign and political risks.

Portfolio Diversification—All the Eggs Not in One Basket

To effectively manage the risks attendant with investing as your investment portfolio grows in value, a sound portfolio diversification through asset allocation principles would need to be employed. The objective of the asset allocation principle is to ensure the portfolio is diversified into different classes of assets, appropriate currencies and maybe also by locations to satisfy your investment objectives and effectively manage the risks associated with the different classes of assets. It allows you participate in different sectors of the economy such that your portfolio is able to bear the upturns and downturns in the different sectors at different times without suffering disproportionate level of losses.

There are three common investment asset classes, each serving best each of the three main investment strategies. Allocating the investible funds amongst these asset classes is considered a crucial part of an investment plan and risk management. Each asset class is better suited for a particular strategy than the other two. Investors typically allocate certain percentages of their portfolio to each asset class. Cash equivalents of short tenor is the class used by investors with a protection strategy; fixed income investments; typically bonds best achieve regular income stream strategy; and investment in businesses and real estate are better suited for a growth strategy. Percentages for each class will vary according to the needs and goals of each investor. A 30 per cent cash, 30 per cent bonds, and 40 per cent shares and real estate allocation model is common, but you might tweak the diversification proportions to fit your own strategy leanings and the dynamics of your financial obligations and objectives.

Insurance

A critical risk management tool that is not usually strategically enlisted is insurance. The tendency is to take out enough insurance to satisfy legislation and to allay that nagging feeling of 'what if'? It is prudent that you keep in view and appropriately insure against the replacement value of any asset that can be lost for any reason if an unexpected and disproportionate depletion in your net worth is to be avoided. Periodical insurance reviews should be carried out to ensure nothing is missed out from the insurance schedule. Synchronising renewal dates or using a spreadsheet to monitor renewals if dates cannot be synchronized will provide a global view and ensure adequate cover of all your insurable assets.

Always Have an Exit Strategy

For any investment, it is good practice to have an exit plan or strategy from the onset. This allows a proper consideration from the onset of the purpose of the investment, the timing and quantum of expected performance that would trigger disposal of part or all of the investment. The biggest advantage of having an exit strategy is its help in ensuring profit opportunities are not missed. Defining and monitoring the exit parameters of an investment makes for good decision making at each opportunity stage. An investor with stipulated profitability and exit timing, for example, is not likely to be tempted and caught out in a volatile market when a crash occurs after a bull run. Most investors that are burnt in the global financial crisis are mostly those with no articulated exit strategy.

Beware Of Financial Advisers Who Also Sell Investment Products

Along with my constant advice that you seek professional help if you are unable to make your own investment analysis and decisions, it is important that a word of caution is added here. No matter who is assisting or providing you financial advice, the responsibility for your finance must remain yours. You must remain in control and have clear objectives of growth and earning to ensure you receive appropriate advice. Financial advisers can sometimes be driven by their product-selling objectives, and you should be aware of their potential conflict with your investment objectives. Their income targets may result in their offering of financial products which do not best serve your portfolio objectives. Watch out; they sell very hard!

Estate Planning—Not a Death Wish

Dealing with the matter of estate planning, by many people who are otherwise intelligent and world-wise, is frequently considered to be premature despite being in middle age. In some cultures discussing the passing on of wealth is viewed as a morbid topic at best or a death wish best left alone. However, the prudent way to view estate planning is that it forms part of the wider topic of financial planning, and on the emotional plane, when a death occurs, those left behind would have been saved further pain and confusion if the financial affairs of the departed has been better organised.

No matter the value of your net worth, it is necessary that a basic estate plan is put in place. A plan would ensure that family financial obligations continue to be met after your demise without a break or anxiety. While we all would rather not consider estate planning before attaining grand old age, things do happen, and it is reasonable to have an orderly plan to pass value to dependents and ensure continuity, that children continue their education as planned and other dependents continue to be looked after.

Ideally, estate planning should be an integral part of your financial plan once you have some value to be passed on to dependents. Estate planning has different elements and tools depending on the particular circumstances, means, and intentions.

The more common of these are the basic will, assigned power of attorney, trusts and family foundations. You should take professional advice and choose the most appropriate of these tools for your particular circumstances. Generally, inheritance can and is usually made difficult by conflict and strife. Discussing estate plans with heirs in the lifetime of the settlor may help prevent disputes and dispel potential conflicts and drawn-out legal actions.

Passing on Legacy—Values beyond Money

'According to the grace of God, which is given unto me, as a wise builder, I have laid the foundation, and another buildeth thereupon.'

—1 Cor. 3:10

According to a survey of their clients, US Trust, subsidiary of a private bank that provides comprehensive wealth management to high net worth and individuals and families found a mere 35 per cent of wealthy individuals believed their children are capable of handling the wealth they will inherit. The majority felt the wealth would likely be a burden or be plundered. The report further said wealth often becomes a burden when a system of values has not passed from parents to children, preventing legacies from being carried on through multiple generations. Legacies are about more than finding tax efficient ways to pass along wealth, it has to be about a legacy of values. Unfortunately, creating this legacy can be complicated by enormous wealth.

'We cannot be too careful in choosing the value system that governs our thoughts and our actions.'

—Benjamin Franklin

The saying "shirtsleeves to shirtsleeves in three generations"- which depicts failure of wealth transmission such that a family could rise out of and plunge back into poverty over only three generations - plays true regularly. This is partly because of the common indiscipline and waste of opportunity when some measure of success has been achieved to be passed on to inheritors. Waste of time and resources usually result from a lack of preparation and discipline, especially of the generations that had some value passed to them and might not have experienced or learnt the discipline of creating and growing value.

There was a disturbing example very widely reported in the American media in July 2015 of a college student who had plundered a $90,000 college trust fund left to her by her grandparents before she could complete her degree. She had gone on a huge spending and travelling spree and was not ashamed to go on a talk show to complain about her parents, who would not come to her rescue. She blamed her parents for not teaching her budgeting earlier in life and how unfair their suggesting she got a job as a precondition if they were to help her with her fees. Some discipline and practical lessons about value earlier on would have kept her grounded and averted the disaster in which she found herself.

The first challenge is recognizing the importance of values in a family's legacy. In establishing a family legacy, the values of those individuals who are passing along wealth are only as viable as their ability to communicate to the next generation and the one after that. It is critical that this happens by creating a 'values statement' that can continue to guide the family for many generations.

Beyond being engaged in the family legacy, the next generation needs to be educated in wealth management. This education is so important that it should start very early, as unprepared heirs have been found to be one of the top reasons financial succession and wealth transfer fail. Many parents are either confused about how much and how early to expose their heirs to their wealth or just don't realise its importance themselves. Failure arises because heirs are usually already exposed to their family wealth through lifestyle, but the greater danger is that they have no idea at all how it all works. This is why most are unable to handle the responsibility, and parents have to plan wealth transmission through appointing a battery of legal and financial professionals designing very complicated documents based on control rather than proper transmission.

The Purpose and Use of Wealth

'The use of riches is better than their possession.'

—Fernando de Rojas

These two quotes talk of responsible use of wealth rather than advocating mindless ostentation or expending on the junk and clutter of lifestyle goods that are never really useful. Ideally, the desirability of working for and having money ought to be predicated on what difference you can make as a result of controlling wealth. Unfortunately, as many do not have such considerations before their ship rolls in, they sometimes plunge straight into the noisy parade of what money can buy for all to see.

The purpose of wealth must be defined for each individual, and it is this definition that influences our attitude towards wealth. Wealth should fundamentally serve to provide for our families' needs and for service to humanity by bringing comfort to others. Often, people appear to live life backwards, spending all their life striving to get wealthy in the hope that they would thereby be made happy and fulfilled. On the contrary, happiness and fulfilment manifest when we commit our talent and resources to service and purpose, a purpose that honours God and humanity and makes a difference in other people's lives. Fulfilment is never achieved from the knowledge of hoarded riches.

When we are granted gifts of wealth, skills, or talent, it is the use to which we put them in furthering good works to inspire and improve community and humanity that makes such talents useful and purposeful. You will find that the joy and fulfilment experienced when you give to good works tends to produce a leverage effect in your own means and the universe does return to you manyfold in different facets of life.

It is wise to understand the place of money as a central means of grace and to always remain considerate of the effects of its use. We must not get carried away by our financial success that we risk forgetting that there is a supreme being who orders the affairs of man, giving us the chances and opportunities. So whether wealth comes by legacy or opportunity, we should remain grateful. Gratitude in itself is a way of giving back.

Chapter 6 – Relationships: Family and Friendships

'Family and friends are hidden treasures; Seek and enjoy their riches.'

—Wanda Hope Cartier

You are created to be relational and not intended to be an island unto yourself. In all spheres of living, relationships are formed whether intended or not, and each relationship will contribute either to a happier state of mind and life or detract from it. Therefore, contributory to a successful and joyful life are the relationships of a person's life and the reverse is also true, unpleasant relationships can create a life of misery.

Family and friendships are the main sources of relating that impact us the most. The influence of family and friends over life from childhood to maturity can affect our well-being, happiness, and even success. For a fulfilling life, these relationships can be managed consciously and intentionally to ensure one enjoys the love, warmth, and loyalty that is usually available within them while minimising the unavoidable emotional stress and negative impacts of conflict that sometimes come with the territory.

Maintaining Your Individuality

The best way of relating is to remain conscious of your separate self such that whatever the nature of a relationship with another, you can take responsibility for yourself and your actions. No one else should dictate how you participate or create your reality through their own actions or thoughts, be it family, spouse, friend or employer. Even in seeking the help of others in a resolving moment of your life, you must ensure you remain a full participant with a veritable position about the matter. We all consciously or subconsciously at some vulnerable times depend on another to be responsible for delivering the thinking for the outcomes we hope or long for. It could seem easier at those stressful moments to abdicate responsibility and rest on our trust of another for thinking through and delivering for our goals in the form of advice; it is however important that you remain conscious of your responsibility and individuality in creating the events and outcomes at such times. Once this matter of your individuality and responsibility is settled, relationships are more nourishing and less stressful or damaging.

Family: You Don't Get to Choose

Family is that body of people affiliated to you by birth, affinity (say marriage), or co-residence and shared nurture (like step-siblings). What we conceive as family can be ambiguous and sometimes confused with the household. The family's function is for giving and receiving care and nurture in a backdrop of mutual obligations and sentimental ties. Your experience of family will shift over time and life stages. As a child, family is where you are first socially and culturally orientated. But the world has moved on from when family mainly served procreation purposes; the fact that producing children is no longer the only function of the family is apparent in many modern-day families where emotional support and the formation of economically sustaining households are clearly of equal importance.

Unlike other relationships, most of family is not by choice. Beyond the point of marriage, when the intending spouses choose each other, they do not get to intentionally select their biological children and the children have no say whatsoever in whom their parents or siblings are. As they say, you just roll with it.

Common Family Setups

Family types are diverse in a wide variety of settings, and their specific functions and meanings depend largely on the social norms in each society. Increasingly changing balance in the roles between parents has affected family setups and family relationships; these have to be consciously managed to avoid malfunction and lack of cohesion.

The nuclear family refers to one of only the parents and their unmarried children. The term is to distinguish between this relatively closer tie and the extended family. The nuclear family is where most of the impact of family is felt and the responsibility lays squarely on parents' shoulders to define and make happen the dynamics that will nurture each member in this very close knit group.

The extended family has a very fluid meaning; it can refer to the kindred network of a few layers of relatives including cousins that extends beyond the nuclear family. How extended this family type is depends on the social structures in particular societies. Different societies and cultures will exhibit some variation in the conception of extended families. Urbanization and migration have very much affected how close or wide the notion of extended means.

There is also now an emergence of what is termed a *blended family* or *stepfamily*, with mixed parents as a result of one or both parents remarried and maybe bringing children of the former family into the new family.

No matter the constitution, the family should be a haven from the world, supplying absolute acceptance and fulfilment. The ideal is for it to be a place of intimacy, love, and trust where we escape the competition and aggressive forces in modern society.

The protective image of the family has waned with increasing individuality as the ideals of family roles keep evolving. Today, the family is becoming more compensatory than protective, supplying what is vitally needed and leaving other social needs to be satisfied outside the family through other relationships. This should not be so, because the family has the earliest and most fundamental impact on us as the main source of values and belief system.

Only one tradition comes close to affecting every human being, and that is the tradition of family. Each of us is shaped, for better or worse, by the upbringing, care, example, and teaching of our parents and family. The underlying sets of beliefs peculiar to each family set the pattern of their interacting and the degree to which members manifest attitudes and values. Hopefully, being mostly a product of your family dynamics, you would generally be happy and secure within your own despite the usual wrangling between siblings and control issues with parents. That should be where you can let down your guard, but you must also be considerate of your role in the family and participate deliberately to create that haven for all members.

Siblinghood and Other Family Interactions

Siblings in a nuclear family have genes in common and spend a good deal of their childhood socializing with one another. This genetic and physical closeness usually result in strong emotional bond, such as love or, unfortunately, in a few instances enmity! The emotional bond between siblings is often complicated and is influenced by many factors such as relative parental treatment, birth order, personality, and personal experiences outside the family. Birth order is commonly believed to have a profound and lasting effect on psychological development and personality of siblings. Firstborn children are generally expected to be conservative and higher achieving, probably because of all that parental discipline on the 'guinea pig'; middle children are natural mediators, while youngest children are usually charming and outgoing since they are likely to enjoy the most relaxed parenting and attention.

There are so many different hypotheses on this matter. In his book *Born to Rebel*, Frank Sulloway argues that firstborn children are likely to be more conscious, more socially dominant, less agreeable, and less open to new ideas compared to their siblings born later. On the other hand, Judith Harris in her reviews suggests that birth order effects may exist only within the context of the family of origin but that they might not be enduring aspects of personality in other contexts of life. None of these beliefs and arguments is sacrosanct as other factors combine to differentiate in each circumstance; however, parents ought to bear in mind the possibility of the contributory effects of family dynamics and birth order on their offspring especially the possibility of damaging sibling rivalry.

Apart from siblinghood, the interrelationship issues that evolve within the family are passively understood by its members even if not openly discussed. It is not unusual, for example, for all in the family (and sometimes outside of it) to know the 'favourite one' who tends to be able to get away with anything. Handling such perceived preferential treatment and finding your own balance between being a team player in the family and being an individual can be a challenging path to tread. It is useful to be mindful of the diversity of temperaments of family members to avoid unnecessary conflict in interacting with other family members.

Of course, the different family structures affect these interactions. It's likely that a strictly nuclear family structure provides a totally different depth and quality of relationship from what might obtain in a blended situation because the changes that blend the family structure as a result of death or divorce exert their own effects on the relationships. For this reason separated and remarried parents especially can have an uphill task of maintaining the bond with their biological children while building a new family. The strain of being torn between maintaining this bond and creating trust in a new configuration can be enormous and if not properly discussed can destroy family members' mutual trust. Understanding early enough the interactions within your family, the differences in temperament, personal motivation and direction, and the way these may affect relating would help you consciously chart your own life path, which may be different from the party line. Ultimately, it is the responsibility of each individual family member to assume an active role and be willing to contribute positively towards the development of both the nuclear and extended family. Awareness of the impact of your role in helping to foster an intimate and healthy family environment that serves as haven to its members is part of living a fulfilling family life.

Friendships—Some Are Closer Than Family

'Of all the things that wisdom provides to help one live one's entire life in happiness, the greatest by far is the possession of friendship'

—Epicurus

The freedom to choose one's friends, unlike family, makes Epicurus's assertion ring true. Friendship is a relationship of mutual affection between people, it is a stronger form of interpersonal bond than in mere acquaintance. Although there are many forms of friendship, the characteristics that make for good friendship include affection, sympathy, empathy, mutual understanding, compassion, enjoyment of each other's company, trust, and the ability to be oneself in expressing one's feelings and able to make mistakes without fear of judgment.

Friendship is sometimes considered as commanding superior emotions than family bonding for the reason that we can choose our friends and are chosen as friends, different from the family relationships for which we have no choice. A. C. Grayling, in his book on friendship, proffers reasons why this might be so. He believes that family bond is weakened in many situations by the complications arising from inheritance, rivalry, and other family conflicts despite which we must remain in family. This notion is buttressed by my observation of siblings that are very different in personal attributes such that it is not imaginable that they would choose each other as friends. In fact, few siblings are also best friends.

By definition, your friends are your favourite people introduced into life through school, work, play, etc. Unlike family, you can choose and 'unchoose' them at will, though some do stick because they continue to intentionally choose you and can make your attempt to 'unchoose' them difficult if not impossible.

The friendships and connections formed through life need not be totally circumstantial; they can be consciously developed and nurtured for mutual satisfaction. For satisfaction to be mutual, we ought to consider our own contribution to the enjoyment of the friendship with another, how we contribute to their happiness and make them keen to keep us as friend. That is what is meant by showing yourself friendly in Proverbs 18: 23.

You Need Good Friends—They Are Good for Your Health

Beyond what the philosophers think about friendship, most research suggests that good friendships enhance an individual's sense of happiness and overall well-being. Indeed, it has been found that strong social support that is present in friendships improve prospects for good health and longevity. Conversely, loneliness and a lack of social support have been linked to an increased risk of heart disease and cancer, as well as higher mortality rates overall. Friendship has even been termed a 'behavioural vaccine' that boosts physical and mental health.

Of course, it must be assumed that it is only friendship of a certain quality that would have these positive health impacts. A number of theories have attempted to explain this correlation between friendship and a person's health status; the most prevalent of these theories holds that good friends encourage their friends to lead healthier lifestyles; encourage their friends to seek and access help when needed; and enhance their friends' coping skills in dealing with illness and other problems. The state of happiness that result from good friendships actually affect physiological pathways that are protective of health.

From experience, we know friendships can have two dimensions: enjoyment and conflict. Only a certain quality of friendship can provide that context where emotional needs are satisfied and activities engaged in intensify pleasure and happiness of friends. Conflicts can arise from a number of situations in friendship usually due to imbalance of sorts that negatively affect mutual benefit or enjoyment of the relationship. Differences in status like marital status and level of achievement can sometimes lead to discomfort. How such imbalance and conflicts are dealt with depends on the quality of the relationship and the personality of the friends. Good friendships tend to develop ways of resolving conflict, ultimately leading to a stronger and healthier relationship in which each friend feels more secure and comfortable with his or her personal identity.

On the contrary, where a friendship is rife with constant or unresolved conflict, it is likely to diminish from rather than contribute to self-esteem and well-being. You should intentionally work at your friendships and be conscious of potential conflicts that might erode your enjoyment of each relationship. A friendship that becomes stressful and diminish your sense of well-being without an easy way to rectify the relationship would not be worth having.

'Observing your close friends will speak volumes about you.'

—Anonymous

While there is no limit to where and with whom one can find friendship, friends tend to share common backgrounds, interests, or demographics. The phrase 'birds of a feather flock together' holds true in most friendships, though there can be friendship fits between people that appear to have different attributes.

Beyond starting a friendship, friends begin to impact and influence each other knowingly or unknowingly. Friendships remain because these mutual impacts and influences are acceptable to both parties, leading to similarities in outlook over time. Observing your close friends speaks volumes about you. Herein lies the danger of taking on a persona or impression purely by association without realizing it. Stay conscious of the reputation your friendships might be bestowing on you, which doesn't only apply to young people. Once a reputation sticks, it becomes very hard if not impossible to change. It is interesting how parents usually seek to sensor their children's friends but the same care is not taken to beam the same sensor on their own friendships. You should constantly ask yourself, what is the plumage of the birds you flock with?

Friendship Needs at Different Stages of Life

I have been friends with Sally for thirty-six years. We met in a postgraduate hall of residence and have lived in different countries ever since. Our lives have taken very different trajectories, and there were times when each of us had been very busy at our profession or raising young families where we would not make contact for a couple of years at a time. However, it appears that at critical points, we somehow find our way back to our friendship. In our middle age, our friendship has blossomed afresh, and I believe one of the winning virtues of our friendship is the long history we have, such that we know each other's stories. That gives us the ability to be ourselves, express our feelings, and make mistakes without fear of judgment. We definitely enhance each other's sense of happiness and overall well-being.

Over a lifetime, friendship needs vary in nature and importance at different stages because of the competing relationships, personal challenges, and other needs. However, friendships are always desirable in varying types and intensity through life to create an enjoyable backdrop to everyday ordinarinesss. A consciousness of your friendship needs at different times and the effect of these relationships on your well-being would help you choose new friends, move away from others, or value some more than others.

In childhood, friendships are often based on the sharing of toys and the enjoyment of shared play. Establishing good friendships at a young age has been found to help a child be better adjusted in society later on in life, having learnt early how to navigate relationships. The advent of preschool playgroups is useful in replacing the neighbourhood playmates and the extended family of yesteryears.

Parents should consciously expose young children to creative and good friendship opportunities for their social engagement. As life progresses, friendships are most important in the emotional life of the adolescent and are often more intense than relationships formed later in life, which is why alumni associations thrive. Parental attention is critical at adolescent friendships because findings indicate that adolescents are less likely to engage in problematic behaviour when their friends did well in school, did not drink, and generally had good mental adjustment.

No surprise that the opposite was found to be the case regarding adolescents who engaged in negative behaviour. This especially strong correlation at this stage of life is perhaps because adolescence is the stage when self-definition comes to most of us. These findings suggest that this key stage – as if managing the effect of their raging hormones is not enough – is when adults in the family have to provide most guidance and be watchful of who their wards are befriending and the extent of their exposure to bad influence. This is sure to be an uphill task because of adolescent resistance to what they consider adult interference, but friendships at this stage clearly have to be under the radar for necessary intervention as necessary.

Adult life events such as marriage, parenting, and career development are sources of new friendships, but they can also interfere with or complicate existing friendships in the transition from young to mature adulthood. After marriage, for example, women and men are likely to have fewer friends of the opposite sex as they take on 'couple' friendships. Adults may also have a challenge in developing or maintaining meaningful friendships in the workplace as work friendships often take on a transactional feel because of competition, such that you need to hide vulnerabilities from colleagues. With work relationships, it is often difficult to know where networking ends and real friendship begins because of possible ramifications on work.

The majority of adults do not make many new close friends once out of college and transitioned to work and family life due to lack of free time to service friendships. It's easy for adults to fall into the thinking that work and family can replace the need for friends. This is not a healthy way to go as good friendships are useful in managing the stress of transitioning into adult responsibilities both at work and at home.

No matter how busy life gets, it is possible to continue to enjoy friendships, even if engagement becomes somewhat intermittent. Anyone about middle age or older will attest to the fact that as family and vocational pressures reduce with age, friendships can again become more important. At this stage, friendships provide the link to the larger community and bring continued societal interaction.

Although older adults tend to prefer familiar and established relationships over new ones, friendship formation can continue well into old age. Older women in particular appear to be able to develop a network of secondary friends – people who may not be intimate but with whom they spend time occasionally, such as a group that meets for lunch or a book club. Generally, older adults who remain in contact with friends tend to show improved psychological and physical well-being. Thankfully, golfing and the like come to the rescue of the men at this stage of life.

Nature of Friendships

Different Mates for Different Purposes

It is important that one is honest and conscious of the nature of each friendship to better engage and enjoy the relationship. Differentiating would help avoid undue expectations or disappointment. In what is termed an agentic relationship (introduced in Milgram's theory, an agentic state is the psychological state a person is in when obeying authority), both parties look to each other for help in achieving practical goals in their personal or professional lives. Agentic friends may help with completing projects, studying for an exam, or supporting each other to achieve similar goals. They value spending time together, but only when it is convenient and there is a need to engage. These relationships typically do not include the sharing of deep emotions or personal information and cannot be expected to serve the purpose of close friendship.

On the other hand, best friends share extremely strong interpersonal ties and tend to affect each other immensely. Such friendships are taken into marriage and other spheres of life and can lead to the development of family friendships. A lot that has been said about the usefulness and quality of friendship in this chapter relate mostly to this close type of relationship. They should be nurtured and valued.

Nonsexual opposite-gender friendships are not always easy to maintain because of suspicion of impropriety, but they can be useful. Having a sounding board of the opposite gender can be very useful for balanced perspectives in a wide variety of situations. Also, peer pressure and rivalries are usually not as pronounced in opposite gender friendships because the friends rarely consider each other as competing peers even when their relationship is based on common pursuits.

Opposite gender friends need to consciously ensure that their partners or spouses remain reassured of the absence of any impropriety.

Team of Rivals—Helping Each Other Excel

'Get in the presence of great people and avoid low-flying people.'

—author unknown

The term 'team of rivals' was made popular by historian and writer Doris Kearns whose book, so named, is about the political style and genius of American president Abraham Lincoln. The point of a friendship with a rival is to learn from each other's proven expertise and personal qualities for the mutual good and improvement of both; as it is said, iron sharpens iron. The only way rivals can make this type of friendship work is for them to avoid demonizing or alienating each other while competing. Once they move beyond say an election, when one of the two is elected, the good that a former opponent can bring to the winner's team should never be wasted as long as both sides can avoid malice and put grudges from the past to rest.

Such maturity was demonstrated by the Lincoln and then mimicked by President Obama when both brought their rivals at elections into critical positions in their cabinets upon winning. The concept is about recognizing and tapping into talents in your rivals that you consider of great quality you can learn from. The virtue is in the ability to co-opt such talent into your team even if you were rivals and may continue to be so in a loose sense of the word. A team of rivals can motivate and make each other continuously improve. Being able to work with rivals is one of the most useful skills for successful leadership, and it takes one with immense confidence to do so.

It is noteworthy to say not all rivals can or should be on your team. A hateful, vengeful, or resentful rival is better left alone as he or she is unlikely to offer any positive impact or contribution to your well-being. For rivals to work together productively, they must have mutual respect for each other and not seek each other's harm, even when they compete. Members of a mastermind group are usually rivals of sorts but are able to come together to brainstorm and arrive at superior solutions than any one alone could. The cooperation and collaboration of the best of the pack is desirable and should be encouraged. Healthy rivalry should never become adversarial as there are strong developmental advantages and help from interacting with rivals.

Ending Friendships

Friendships end for many reasons. Sometimes friends move away and are forced to relate less due to the distance. In family friendships divorce can cause an end to friendships, as people drop one or both of the divorcing couple. At the younger adult stage, friendships may end as a result of entry into new social groups as would happen when one friend goes to college and the other does not. Friendships may end by fading quietly away where the relationship has reduced in significance to one or both friends or it has become increasingly stressful. They may also end abruptly due to some irreconcilable conflict. How and whether to talk about the end of a friendship is a matter of etiquette that depends on the quality of the relationship, circumstances, and the people involved. Discussions are usually only necessary if a remedial intervention is desired or considered productive. Usually an acrimonious end to a friendship does not require a debriefing session.

JUST
MARRiED

Chapter 7 - Marriage: Grace to Choose Aright

'There is no greater risk than matrimony, but there is nothing happier than a happy marriage.'

—Benjamin Disraeli

I have come to glean some interesting insight into the institution of marriage through observation, counselling, and of course forty years of personal experience. If I were to review the status of some of the marriages that took off from the starting block more than thirty five years ago, mine included, the success rate, to which thankfully mine contributes, is not exciting although there are a myriad of shades of success, depending on who you are talking to. I can't help but wonder why many happen unto marriage, usually possessing very little under-standing of the nature of the institution

A man I counselled a few years ago and his wife of thirty years still live together. However, they are rarely seen together at functions or just about anywhere. When you ask one about the other, you get a polite 'fine' in response before they either beat a quick retreat or change subjects. Telling is the fact that one of their grown-up children refused to be married at their family church because, in her words, "If the church wants to pretend that my parents are still married, then I don't want any of that model of marriage". You can draw your own conclusions!

Another couple I have observed from a distance actually show up together but are always taking a swipe at each other in public, to the embarrassment of innocent bystanders. I can't help wondering why they are still together or come out together.

And then there is the 'society' couple; – all seem fine in this marriage; apart from the fact of the husband being a functioning alcoholic about which the wife does not appear to mind or care. They show up well and appear quite friendly with each other despite the occasional public embarrassment, but it is obvious his alcoholism and her lack of concern or attention are symptoms of some dire situations in their family concerning the state of their finances and interrelating issues.

These three examples are counted among the successes while many who started with us off the block have simply packed up their unions due to irreconcilable differences. So what can I tell you about marriage and how to consciously navigate its waters of human-eating creatures?

So Why Bother?

There are many different opinions about the purpose of marriage or reasons to tie the knot, but the simple one by an anonymous sage kind of sums it up for me: "Sometimes life is too hard to be alone, and sometimes life is just too good to be alone".

People marry for many different and combinations of reasons, including legal requirements, spiritual and religious dictates, social norms, emotional satisfaction from a public declaration of commitment, location and protection of children, and economic consolidation. In some cultures the act of marriage can create obligations that extend beyond the wedded parties to their extended family members.

Ultimately, people get married because marriage is beneficial in many ways – a good marriage, that is. Research confirms that being accountable for and to another person results in both parties living more responsible, productive, and satisfying lives, which translates to less depression, anxiety, and stress. I would say very good reasons indeed to go for it!

However, tarry a bit, girls, because going by a study used by Elizabeth Gilbert in her book *Committed*, there is proof that this advantage is loaded more to the advantage of the menfolk. Married men are less likely to be afflicted by chronic illnesses like heart disease and diabetes than their singleton mates. Worrisome is the fact that the study shows that the converse appears to be true for women: they found that married women fare worse than their single sisters!

The study concluded that married women might be more prone to suffering from those same diseases because of the 'women are from Venus' emotional tendency, which affects their expectations from marriage and their spouses. The other culprit that might be causing this imbalance is the hardship of bearing a disproportional burden of housekeeping and childrearing by women. This burden, thankfully, is slowly being redressed with the increasing education and independence of women. So if the girls could borrow a few leaves from Mars (from where men are supposed to originate) and be more rational in managing their expectations of marriage and spouse, they should not be fearful of marriage.

Historical and Cultural Antecedents of Marriage

To gain better perspective and understanding of marriage, it is enlightening to go back to its origins. While time and modernity might have changed the details and some expectations of marriage, its historical and religious antecedents still shed some light and provide wisdom to better understand and navigate the institution. Marriage has two dimensions: one is sociolegal, which amounts to a tripartite contract between a man, a woman, and the state or God. The other is the long-term voluntary commitment by two people who, because of their affection for each other, wish to pool resources and share the joys and burdens of life. This second dimension means it is about choice, affection, and sharing.

Historically, the roots of marriage were mainly for social order. The first objective of marriage was to constrain women's sexuality to one household to avoid unruly engagement between the sexes so that men could be sure they were bequeathing their property and wealth to their own offspring.

The second root was simple financial expediency, allowing men to build households of wives and children to support their planned growth in farming or whatever their business was that required the labour of many hands before the advent of slaves and servants. Also, in medieval Christianity, marriage existed for the religious views about women's sexuality outside wedlock and social views about wealth. It is noteworthy that it was only in the eighteenth century, when the poorer classes began acquiring property, that the requirements of legal forms of marriage were extended to them too.

It appears the social order purpose of making ancestry and property traceable was at the foundation of religious injunction to marry. These antecedents show that the institution was originated to satisfy societal needs for orderliness in the relating of both sexes for the benefit of society and to avoid complication and confusion arising from indiscriminate engagements. Marriage rules and vows evolved in each society to support its expectations of social organization. Many Indigenous societies were mainly polygamous for similar social reasons.

This background is not to make you cynical and devoid of romantic expectations of marriage; it's only an attempt to encourage engagement beyond just physical attraction and romance as a basis for this important relationship that should be for the long haul. It is to encourage courting parties to ensure there is the possibility of a platonic companionship that is better suited to support the many unromantic matters like procreation, parenting, financial security and other life issues that marriage is expected to take in its stride. It is easier to resolve and jointly manage these tedious aspects where a pleasant companionship exists and there is respect and trust for each other's opinion and life view. It is to bring home the fundamental fact that the 'love, crazy love' period of romance when infatuation is mainly in play, does simmer down over time, and it's good to ensure there is a good companionable place to which it can simmer down, rather than to nothingness or a break-up.

Making the Big Decision—And the Grace to Choose Right

It would be nice if there was a working formula for choosing a spouse or some articulated basis for the choice. Apart from cultures where it is believed that such an important and far-reaching decision ought not to be left to young people with little experience of how the marital life works, the rest of us are left to make this decision by ourselves. Many, while still almost children, take this step while juggling other matters like career, money, and being responsible for self for the first time.

Help Meet is Who you Need

Without a doubt, consciously planning and living an orderly and fulfilling life for your singular self is a good foundation for progressing to finding a partnership that will fit and perhaps enhance such a life over time. It is easier to identify a complementing spouse if you already have a reasonable idea of your planned future and the kind of person that would fit the role of partner for your journey. As marriage requires the integration of two different lives that would have evolved sometimes differently through childhood and young adulthood, a reasonable fit is easier between two people who already possess individual self-knowledge and are sure of the partnership they need for their future.

'Help meet' is how the Holy Bible depicts who one should marry – that person that is equipped to provide the help or complementary attributes that would satisfy the needs of one's life and thereby enrich it. Many people miss their help meet because they are yet to decipher their own personality, life direction, and needs from a spouse before they happen to marry someone.

Regularly, life partner choices are based on just physical beauty, popularity, or social standing to the disappointment of one or both parties. Imagine the surprise in store for someone, maybe soon after the wedding bells, who really just wants to concentrate on building a serious career and a well organised homestead when he or she fails to get the desired support and environment from a social butterfly spouse. When I hear such a one bemoan his or her frustration, I wonder, sometimes aloud, how this person could have expected the lively party animal he or she married to suddenly want to settle down to what would seem like a 'boring' lifestyle.

In seeking a help meet, think who would provide the backdrop or nourishing environment for the life of your dreams – whose traits and character would not be a distraction or impediment to how you wish to live life but rather complement your strengths and weaknesses; who you would continue to be proud to call your spouse as years roll by; who would continue to make you bounce in the direction of your desired destination. If, for example, being intellectually engaged is what would enrich your life, there would be trouble ahead if you already know that such stimulation would not be available from who you plan to marry. The help meet concept is a two-way street, so you should consider your own role and fit as help meet in your partner's life in the same detail. Marriage is a social union or legal contract between two people that should create a kinship and intimacy in a variety of ways. Beyond all that, they should be the help meet to each other.

The Pitfall in Choosing

Apparently, the main culprit to your decisions regarding all things romantic is the hormone called dopamine, the pleasure chemical to blame for that out-of-control, addictive, and vulnerable feeling you experience in fresh love. Dopamine controls the brain's pleasure centres and regulates emotional responses, and much too much of it is secreted when romance hits.

Unfortunately, coming up a distant and quieter second is the practical consideration of how compatible you are with your amour and how sustainable your newfound love is. When such a life-changing decision is being made by a young person, to whom all things appear simple and possible, dopamine can only further fuel his or her impulsive temperament. Achieving a good balance between practicality and the hormones is the major challenge here since sensibility and sensuality don't always travel well together.

The philosophers, from the stoics to the epicureans, all warn about the danger of sensual love predicating important relationships. And what relationship, if I may ask, is more important and in need of a rock-solid foundation than the institution of marriage? It was the need of distinguishing between truth (reality) and fiction (dopamine-fuelled) and tempering the latter with the former that led to Plato's conception of love known as the platonic relationship, which is generally misunderstood to preclude romance. He said the physical sense cannot fully grasp the essence of things. It only sees the way things look on the outside and, therefore, can usually lead you to a wrong conclusion about things.

For instance, a well-dressed and handsome man may actually not be a good person inside and could turn abusive with little provocation; the senses have no way of telling you this. The so-called sixth sense may do so, but certainly not the eyes, ears, and touch. They only perceive the appearance and will mislead the person who trusts solely in them. To predicate a marriage choice on only the senses is to equate good looks with inner goodness. So when a smitten person says, "I know this person" because of the physical appearance, he or she might not really know the other person and then claim to love who is not fully known. A marriage decision based on this type of perception tends to spell some trouble ahead!

However, if you're patient to establish a relationship based on actual inner qualities and focus on higher values, the result is more likely to be a stable relationship based on greater consideration for one another apart from physical attraction.

'It is not a lack of love but a lack of friendship that makes unhappy marriages.'

—Friedrich Nietzsche

Am I asking then that you ignore sexual and sensual attraction in seeking a marriage partner? Definitely not. Some physical attraction and sensuality are required for an exciting courtship to occur in the first place. The advice is that you understand the weakness in expecting only sensual love to sustain a relationship that would service so many practical and sometimes rigorous aspects life. It is wiser that you ensure your marriage decision is anchored on a friendship love that is mentally fulfilling and satisfying and is based on a shared outlook about life in general. If this is not the case, it is unlikely or difficult to achieve a wide-based relationship in which you and your significant other can formulate and commit to a joint life with agreed-upon goals.

Love based on friendship comes with kindness, respect, and belief in the other person. The personal security and mental stability enjoyed in that kind of relationship is the reason you stay and evolve together. The relationship becomes a valuable part of your life that you would not risk but rather nurture. It is also of great importance that you bring into the relationship what would delight the other to make them continue to stay and commit to a joint life with you. Different people desire or require a different combination of attributes in a partner for what they consider to be a good marriage, you need to discuss these sincerely beforehand, to avoid unrealistic expectations that become the complain list after the marriage knot has been tied.

For the record, the platonic type of relationship, if allowed to develop, does not preclude romance and the begetting of children. A marriage evolving therefrom would be on a firmer foundation. Ultimately, the risk of getting wrong what might be the most pivotal decision of your life is a scary prospect because an error in this choice can make life askew, with a very slim hope of realignment once marriage commences.

In the game of life, we cannot choose everything simultaneously and therefore need to place weights on our options to choose right where it is most critical. In very few aspects of life does choosing wrong come back to haunt us more than in the choice of a marriage partner. A lot of weight should be placed on this decision, and the grace to choose right is worth praying for.

Get Counsel

As an investment in your future, you should endeavour to have a no-holds-barred discussion with an experienced counsellor before a final commitment to marriage. I observe that the cultures that have maintained the traditional help and involvement of the family in making this decision appear to have been mostly saved the subsequent pain, confusion, and long-term effects of marriage breakdowns that have become common in less traditional societies. This, by any stretch of imagination, is not advocacy for the matching and forcing of a mate on a young person by a controlling family, because the repercussions of that can be unsavoury or even tragic. Rather, the suggestion is for a wholesome involvement and help of your closest and dearest in making this defining decision. It need not be a parent that provides this loving guidance, someone whose values and opinion you respect, that you can trust and fully disclose your concerns to is who is needed for the job. It could be a sibling, or a very close friend. Consider good counselling as a risk-management tool in managing the dopamine pumping effect that obliterates all reason and wisdom when you have this decision to make. By the way, a long courtship does not preclude the use of counsel as anyone who has been married for any considerable time will tell you that courtship aren't nothing like the real thing. The real thing involves children, work, personal idiosyncrasies hitherto masked or thought to be cute but which become less adorable at close range! Get some guidance from those who have been through the real thing.

Time to Marry!

'For everything there is a season... a time to embrace... a time to love.'

—Ecclesiastes 3: 1–8

What would you say is a good age for a person to marry? The popular opinion is about 27 years old, give or take a few years. Statistics show that women first marry about this age while men wait a bit longer. Several studies suggest that people that marry in their early twenties are twice as likely to divorce their spouse at some point in their life. This might be because they may have tied the knot for the wrong reasons or did not possess the self-realization and maturity to manage the transition that marriage requires. In reality, there are people in their twenties that have achieved self-realization and are capable of handling marriage while some much older people are yet to know what their own self are about. It all depends on the readiness of each person; for those who still have some way to go in self-discovery and life direction, a hold on the marriage decision would be a good idea. If, on the other hand, you are already secure with self and have made the marriage decision responsibly, then get on with it!

Delaying marriage, especially if you have been in courtship for two or more years, simply because career and enjoying your youth loom large while settling down appears to be a boring thing to do, you might want to think again. You need to bear in mind the impossibility of choosing all roads simultaneously and seriously consider the biological clock and other life intentions that gain from settling down with the right spouse at the right time. Later matrimony does work out for some people, but many, as a result of leaving it too late, do 'miss the boat', which can create a major imbalance in later life.

Generally, there are early starter advantages: clarity of life direction, childbearing, and financial goal setting are the obvious gains of settling down with the right partner as soon as you are ready. The tick-tock of the biological clock make the ideal timing of marriage sooner for girls who are interested in procreation. It is considered that birthing is ideal before 30, and while the lads might not have to worry for a few years, but they too cannot totally ignore the biological clock.

Of particular concern regarding timing is what I consider to be the possibility of missing one's own boat. Young people, especially the very attractive, popular, or successful tend to become very choosy and consider no one good enough or deserving of them. This is a dangerous attitude that can make them stay unattached, albeit unintentionally, until it is too late. (By too late I mean they can then fall into a period when it becomes difficult to meet possible partners for the reason of age and shrinking society engagement.) I advise that young people keep this risk in mind and not take themselves unduly seriously relative to other people. Too many people have voiced to me their regret regarding this error, but realization usually come too late in life.

The Marriage Experience... Achieving Success.

In giving Adam a woman, according to the Holy Bible, God said it was not good for man to be alone. God's concerns must have been the man's need for a fully trusting companionship, his need for a friend to play with, to joke with, and to bounce ideas by; a mate for empathy and help; and of course, for the begetting of children. Any marriage veteran would affirm that marriages only fail for lack of friendship, empathy, and kindness and that the marriage experience benefits immensely from pleasant companionship.

The Role of Expectation

Expectations from marriage can differ somewhat in diverse cultures, and the expectations of both parties affect the probability of success in matrimony. Your own expectations and those of your intended spouse need to be synchronised beforehand through discussions and negotiations if misunderstanding and disappointment were to be avoided later. In the book *Committed*, Ms Gilbert interviewed people of different ethnic groups and found, for example, that among the Vietnamese Hmong, though they fall in love in the usual way that we know it, it is not believed that is the sole basis or central purpose for marriage. The Hmong know the clear-cut roles of each party to the union and failure in those roles would earn community scorn.

She noted that even in the West, until not too long ago, people engaged in what might be termed pragmatic marriages. When interviewed, her elderly Connecticut neighbours could not dredge up a romantic memory about the origins of their marriage. Mr Webster got married to Mrs Webster because he was soon to be taking over the family farm and having been instructed by his brother to get himself a wife as, 'You cannot run a proper farm without a wife', and he did.

Mr Webster settled for Lillian because, in his words, 'She was the right one, she was nice, she was healthy, she was good, and she would do'. She 'would do' should not be taken as solely utilitarian; it means she was the right one for his life: help meet. Although the origin of their marriage was not that of a passionately fevered love, Ms Gilbert attests to the fact that their marriage was definitely not a loveless one. She bears testimony to the care, tenderness, and yes, love, between the two.

Apparently, the Hmong, the Websters, and other knowing folks expect marriage as the cooperation of co-pilots on what is usually an initially little-understood project called life. This pragmatic view is definitely a useful context for managing the 'expectation checklist' of anyone hoping for success in matrimony.

Your expectations as you approach marriage and decide on the partner to put down sail with will make a lot of difference in choosing right and making a success of it. The Hmong are not taught to expect that their spouse's job was to make them blissfully happy all the time. Rather, they are taught that their own role in marriage is important and would be relied upon by all connected to both spouses. Not having such undue expectation, they do not easily reap disenchantment from marriage. Because of their view, the Hmong may in fact be blessed with the gift of certainty; that of having only one path set before them that makes them confident that they are on the correct path which they tread without hesitation.

A marriage choice should not be seen as devoid of romance just because it entails a careful consideration of whether what one desires and needs for a fulfilled life is available in marriage to a particular person. Mr Webster had most likely known the young Lilian all his life, and something of her person must have attracted him such that when the time came, he knew she would fit the mould.

Beyond making the decision about the particular person to pitch tent with, your expectation, or non-expectation (most people do not think past the wedding arrangement and ceremony) of the marriage experience continues to dictate how successful and satisfying you will find it to be. It is often said that marriage is hard work. It is likely that what can really be hard work is life itself and marriage only becomes hard work when predicated wrongly within life. Marriage is bound to be hard work if you expect all of your life's joy and happiness to derive from another person just because you are married to him or her. How more dangerous can modern expectation of matrimony be if a recent survey of young women found that they expect a husband to be the one to inspire them.

Compare that to the expectation of women of same age back in the 1920s, who were looking for 'a man who is decent, honest, kind, and with the ability to provide for his family'. You could argue that expectations are bound to change over time as women have become more confident and no longer rely on men to provide for them, but the problems that can emanate from marrying a passionate man who cannot be said to be decent, honest, kind, and able to provide for his family are enormous! Problems are also bound to attend marriage to a beautiful woman who cannot be said to be nice, good, focussed, and industrious, as I am sure Mrs Webster was.

The central message here is for you to be careful not to expect askew or too much of marriage. Increasingly, it appears that the breakdown of marriages is because many seek to load a far heavier cargo of expectations onto the creaky old boat of matrimony than the vessel was ever built to bear in the first place. Just like the Hmong women did, and I believe as any wise modern person does, you can find other contributors to happiness from your network of family, friends, and extended community. If you are not to reap immense disappointment, it is advisable not to expect marriage to be a device for delivering ultimate bliss. I sometimes wonder why other relationships that are just as important are not burdened with that level of expectations; not family, not friendship. Expecting or seeking another person to complete you and be solely responsible for your joy and inspiration can only put undue emotional pressure on that person and the relationship. What would be delightful is the coming together of two whole persons, not seeking affirmation or purpose from a partner, to create an enjoyable and fulfilling relationship.

Balancing the burden of domesticity is an area that should be discussed and negotiated ahead because the expectations of both partners can be poles apart because of different experiences of their culture or family. The disproportionate burden on married women because of childcare especially must be part of that conversation.

Themes about Marriage of Which to Be Mindful.

Defined by Matrimony

Marriage is frequently entered into without much thought of its implications and affectations on the lives of the two people involved. Rarely is consideration given to how a marriage might affect or even change the direction of each spouse's life.

Marriage is defining; it should be expected to be a defining or redefining experience to an appreciable extent. Even when a marriage has ended, there seems to be a need to use the letters BM and AM (before marriage and after marriage) in the location of events in the life of the divorced parties. If you talk to those who have been married more than once or divorced from just one marriage, they have such clarity about the timing of events in relation to each marriage. Marriage, no matter if happy, un-engaging or unhappy, significantly impacts many aspects of the participants' lives.

Your social engagement, finance and financial obligations, forms of recreation – the list is endless – are all impacted by marriage. A married person can no longer be fully available in other relationships like friendship and family as before. It's as if marriage places its participants on a kind of leash, whether they believe it or not. The existence of children increases that impact such that there is a continuing effect long after a marriage is over; celebrations and problems concerning those children continue to be shared, and the opportunity for relating by the parents never really ends. This phenomenon relating to children then affects a subsequent marriage or relationship of divorced spouses. Marriages are highly and maybe permanently defining, and you ought to be mindful of this before the wedding plans commence.

Thirty-five years after I tied the knot, with not much thought then for the likely turns on the road of life, I have since found that the single fact that I got married has dictated my geographical locations and moves in a major way. It is generally assumed that this phenomenon is usually truer for a wife than for a husband, but that only depends on the culture in which a marriage exists. A man's life can be as much affected and its direction as much influenced by whom he marries. A man's happiness and success in building a good life can be dependent on the personality and support of the wife he chooses to marry.

Although I am a strong proponent of the principle that each of us is responsible for the outcome of our lives and staunchly disagree with blaming another for one's failure, I have found that many people are significantly defined by who they have married or how that marriage played out. The quality of upbringing that your children get will be hugely influenced by your spouse's outlook and personal traits no matter how effective you are in that department. The sheer effort to minimise another's influence in that kind of situation with the attendant constant disagreement will affect each spouse's life, and in this case, their children's. The marriage decision is definitely a big opportunity for each person, the opportunity to intentionally define your life direction by your choice, and judgment in that all important matter of a life partner. Hopefully for good.

A Study in Cooperation, Autonomy, and Containment—The Porcupine Dance.

The need for two individuals who have grown up in different families and sometimes cultures to achieve civil and peaceful coexistence has been likened to the porcupine dance cycle. To avoid freezing, these prickly animals bundle together to provide warmth, but once the critical and comfortable warmth level is achieved, they become irritatingly aware of the painful poking of each others' quills and by reflex separate. However, no sooner have they separated when the chills send them back into each other's embrace.

This is a good metaphor for the need for cooperation and negotiation of important matters, especially at the onset of matrimony. In matters concerning raising of children, handling money, career location moves, and the seemingly inconsequential issues like the choice of furniture, family diet, and vacation, spouses can be said to be involved in a form of porcupine dance; embracing, separating to disagree, negotiating, and embracing again even after being married for decades.

You should expect to continually seek the elusive balance between personal autonomy and matrimonial cooperation, especially if you are married to a confident individual with strong positions. Unfortunately, one party can sometimes compromise away in this process some precious aspects of his or her personality that is needed to be happier and more fulfilled. Each couple – in fact, each person – would have to learn his or her own choreography of the porcupine dance and compromise to ensure each remains fulfilled and not totally subsumed in satisfying the other. This synchronization of two lives usually means some taming or containment of the freedom of each spouse's life in compromises. Synchronisation is made more difficult the more autonomy a person is accustomed to before marriage and for how long he or she had only himself or herself to please in the singlestate.

The need for compromise that results in some containment of each spouse is sometimes viewed from a negative aspect as control and submission, but containment, if voluntary, can be beneficial. Both spouses in a marriage are contained by their marriage vows. Having to consider another in your actions and decisions is already containment. Heading home rather than to drinks after work, and saving for family expenditure instead of impulsive spending are nothing if not containment. Of containment comes discipline, doing right and being a less selfish person. Containment introduces some structure and boundaries, curbing excesses that could otherwise rob a life of orderliness and success. The modern aspiration of 'having it all' can lead to the mistaken belief that we can achieve equal parts autonomy and intimacy in marriage, and to seek to achieve marriages that empower, enable, fulfil without some compromise and containment. The cooperation and autonomy balance is a thin path to walk but getting it right yields peaceable coexistence that is needed as conducive backdrop to a good marriage.

Harnessing Individual Talents in Marriage

The two are meant to come together and become one, with a common purpose and destiny. That is what the marriage vows imply, and that is the expectation of most societies and spouses. However, how do individual talents that have been honed for most of each partner's lifetime blend into this expectation and what are the challenges that face a union of strong and talented individuals? Such individuality must not be allowed to stand in the way of a good marriage neither should individual talents be wasted or undermined by the lack of reasonable cooperation and confidence. What is important and necessary is open communication and understanding by the parties before their commitment to paddle one boat together.

There could be individual strengths that can be harnessed for the benefit of the family, and it would be a shame to waste such benefits. If a couple is able to recognize and understand why and when a task is not a family expedition and is better accomplished by entrusting it to the one with the requisite skills; the resulting division of labour according to individual strengths and talent would be to the benefit of the family. As long as mutual trust and respect ensures each party is comfortable, the state of the union can only be stronger for it.

There are men who are exceptional parents and are naturally better equipped than their wives in some aspects of parenting. It would be a shame to let their children miss out on this gift just because it is not the norm for fathers to attend parent/teacher meetings. My own father was particularly hands-on about parenting; he was fully involved with his children's clothes, discipline, and especially our education. His extraordinary parenting skills have had long-lasting effects on me.

On the other hand, the skills of a wife that is adept at negotiating and planning should not be wasted just because we think those are skills for the male.

A loss of individuality that results in stifling and loss of fulfilment for the reason of marriage is likely to have far reaching negative consequences for an individual and indeed the union, and this need not be the case.

Endurance, Not Long-suffering

'The state of marriage is one that requires more virtue and constancy than any other. It is a perpetual exercise in mortification.'

—St Francis de Sales.

In pondering how some people actually live out their marriage, it appears that they ought to ask themselves if they have considered the realities and are committed to be married to another – for better or worse. Many appear not to understand or possess the patience that is required to abide in marriage. Patience is a virtue that is most relevant in marriage whether you are male or female. It is only natural to enjoy being in love – the excitement and the flush of new love, the feeling of having found a special person and all that. Unfortunately, the story does not end there; those who expect marriage to be more of all that soon find that their spouses would sometimes not be at their most reasonable, or most attractive. The occasional sickness or everyday ordinariness (very different from the pruned and groomed state exposed to each other on dates) does happen, and such people may get impatient and are too quickly irritated and disappointed within months of marriage. To them, such are not matters to be patient about and worked at, but the excuse to complain to everyone at earshot or to bail out!

There is a need for patience and reasonable endurance in living with another person if stability were to take footing. You should consider the changes the other person has to endure by living with you and the autonomy they are yielding as a result of becoming one with you. Endurance is predicated on and helped by kindness and fairness to one's spouse and you must make the effort at some endurance.

There are, of course, boundaries a person should not be expected to cross in the name of marital understanding and endurance. Abuse in any form and flagrant adultery are inexcusable and are too damaging to expect a spouse to endure. Abuse, whether physical or psychological, is a pointer that the abuser needs help, and that is what he or she should get. Help will forestall impending disaster in an abusive relationship for both parties as is shown by cases of spousal abuse that become fatal. Usually, a belated regret resonates that an abusive spouse should have sought psychological help that would have averted tragedy. There is absolutely no use to sacrificing one spouse under the charade of keeping a marriage afloat. Also, flagrant adultery, as opposed to a one-off situation that can be resolved and forgiven, is disrespectful and damaging to the self-esteem of the suffering spouse. Neither abuse nor flagrant adultery should be endured. Endurance, not long suffering, helps a marriage.

Money in Marriage

Putting finances at the bottom of the marriage agenda can be a costly mistake. A 2011 survey by Utah State University in the United States found that a different money attitude in spouses is one of the biggest relationship breakers out there. Very few marital problems compete with money and poverty in destroying marriages. Poverty and lack breed extreme tension while money can provide options which, if not available, make life tedious. Options like childcare or a vacation can dissipate brewing tension, making life bearable and reduce hopelessness that could easily lead to failure.

You should expect to deal with money challenges in marriage (and not necessarily because of a shortage of the stuff). Most separated or divorced adults say they wished they had discussed money before and during their marriage. Shying away from discussing money is a dangerous development, because one or both parties could be bottling up resentment that would then affect trust and cooperation in the union. Talking about money is as important as the "Are we going to have children and how many?" discussion.

If there are different money attitudes and values, these should be reconciled. There are telling ways to ensure your values about money are on the same page with your intended's outlook even before you tie the knot. Playful conversations or careful observation can easily expose your future spouse's money values. A simple one is to imagine you have won a million dollars in cash and asking each other what you would do with that money. The answers will offer instant insight into any differences in attitudes towards finances. If one of you is a penny pincher that hoards every penny while the other is an extravagant spender, this would be a good time to address those differences. Discussing your dreams and seeing if they can be integrated to forge a realistic financial plan for reaching your joint goals would also be a pointer to your individual money personalities. It is only when you have nailed down your attitudes to money and dealt with differences that you can develop a financial plan for a future together.

The Matter of Joint Accounts

Today's socioeconomic structures mean that most households require more than one income to sustain a decent standard of living and build a secure financial future for the family. Forward planning and good communication would help a couple avoid unnecessary financial tension and frustration resulting from the necessary sharing of financial responsibilities. One of the frequent but fragile money matters in marriage is that of whether to operate a joint account. The shared expenses of food, utility bills, rent or mortgage payments, school fees, and family vacations would require some form of joint finance to be worked out as long as there is more than one income. If one person earns significantly more or less than the other, it would be fair to contribute amounts in proportion to reflect this.

However, joint financing of expenses and obligations is not necessarily synonymous with running a joint account, and spouses may be better off managing their accounts separately to avoid undue conflict. If, for example, one spouse is less disciplined with spending or one perceives a joint account as either too restrictive or infringing on their independence, it is probably better to have separate accounts until such concerns are laid to rest and trust built. What is critical is to consciously keep the big financial picture of the family in mind whether finances are managed separately or jointly. Unfortunately, keeping totally separate finances without open communication may result in each spouse making individual financial decisions that are not in synergy with or at the detriment of the family's long-term goals.

A good compromise or alternative to fully joint accounts could be maintaining a special joint account contributed to for certain large and recurring expenses. Alternatively, particular expenses could be assigned for settlement by each party as their contribution to the family budget. This is a popular model that allows each spouse to take some responsibility in maintaining the household while retaining some financial autonomy. There is no perfect answer to the joint-versus-separate accounts debate; there are various hybrids, and you have to consider your situation and circumstances to work out what is best and comfortable for your family.

A word of caution though regarding joint accounts: there is usually some confusion about the difference between a joint account holder and an additional signatory. Creditors view a joint account as they would an individual account, this means that each account holder is financially liable, and of course either party can withdraw at will. A principal account holder spouse can however make the other an authorized signatory, not a joint account holder.

It is important to note that whilst an authorized signatory is able to operate the account, there is usually a limit to the activities they are allowed, and the main account holder can choose to remove or change the basis of their access at any point. Most importantly, if the main account holder were to die, the other signatory to the account would immediately cease to have access to money in that account as it becomes part of the deceased's estate. Depending on the fine print, some fully joint accounts can suffer this shutdown of access to funds once knowledge of the demise of one party is known to the bank. This may be a good reason why each spouse should have access to some money out of the joint purse.

Challenges in Marriage, Not Insurmountable

The level of tedium that a person experiences in close relationships like marriage can be self inflicted. Such hardship could result solely from how you choose to react to the actions of the other in the relationship. Granted, a goal-oriented person would suffer some frustration in a marriage to someone with a less driven disposition, but such frustration must be seen not only in light of the one whose action or personality frustrates you but as a result of the impatience and intolerance that your own expectation burdens you with. There is also the measure of your commitment (or absence of it) to the long-term view of the relationship which affects how much work you are willing to put into making it work through communication and compromise. If you are not constantly considering the option of divorce or separation, it is amazing how resolution options emerge. Most of the challenges in marriage and their resolution depend on spouses managing their individual attitudes, expectations, reactions, and contribution to conflicts. It is useful to bear this in mind long before such conflicts arise.

Differences in Culture or Family Background

In what is increasingly a global village, cross sociocultural marriages will occur. If you decide to marry a person of a different social background or culture, and you both are unable or unwilling to sensitively integrate your family or cultural differences, it can become a huge source of stress, especially if not properly acknowledged and commitments extracted at the onset. Young people, in the flush of fresh love, are wont to believe love conquers all differences and think they can dispense with extended family and friends once they find the love of their life. Seriously, why should you need or have to discard or replace the life you have always known? Your new family ought to be an offshoot of the old and should allow you continue to enjoy your history and antecedents. Also, your children should not be robbed of their extended family ties and relationships that would contribute to their own sense of identity in future.

The implications of differences even when you have emerged to 'world citizenship' must not be underestimated. Early life experiences, with their lasting effects, show up soon enough. Our origins call back to us at unexpected stages of life, and we can surprise even ourselves by the taste preferences and affectations from our antecedents.

Studies have shown that commonality in social and cultural backgrounds, education, and economic classes, plus the support of family, are factors that have been identified as predisposing to a healthy and satisfying marriage. You therefore need very deep thought and a no-holds-barred consideration and discussion before embarking on a cross-cultural union.

The young Kenyan woman I mentioned in the preface was perhaps a victim of rushing into a cross-cultural marriage just to find out soon enough that she really did not fully know her man and his cultural affectations. It is the surprise element that causes resentment or irreconcilable conflict. If full attention was paid beforehand to possible trouble down the road, time and effort would have been made to better discover each other, including the wider implications and commitment of marrying into each other's family and culture.

Family, In-laws, and Friends

Having recommended and encouraged the caring role of family and friends in counselling and supporting couples to achieve a good marriage, I must warn of the unpleasant underbelly of bad counsel, meddling, and participation of friends and family, usually with good intentions in your marriage. Although the interference by in-laws has the pride of place as one of the common reasons for the breakdown of marriages, friends and a multitude of counsellors can be more lethal. It is normal that you would share your concerns about brewing marital problems with a trusted one and are likely to be given counsel on how to proceed. You must filter such advice through your own better knowledge of your spouse and the deeper roots of your problem. Other parties, whether family or friends, simply cannot know the full backstory to your issues. Furthermore, you must take ownership for how you apply counsel that you might receive and ultimately take responsibility for your decisions and actions. In the end, the two people to best work out a marital problem are the two who know the full story: you and your partner.

The African cultural posture to the in-law matter is that a marriage is in fact a union of two families rather than two lovebirds. An African marriage is never an island of groom, bride, and their children in a nuclear family. The in-laws are usually well researched ahead of marriage; the state of the family one marries into is considered a good indication of what to expect of the marriage about to be contracted. I have never understood the initial posture of many young people about their in-laws when it is from thence came their very much loved new spouse. Bear in mind that your relationship with the in-laws is a two-way street that is usually clogged with suspicion and understandable anxiety. You are anxious of their interference and influence on your spouse; the in-laws are anxious in return about your influence and are full of concern that they might lose a hitherto family member to his or her new spouse. It needs not be so as the in-laws can and should be a good resource of extended family relationships with you and your children. I have fortunately enjoyed a trusting and loving relationship with both my mother-in-law of blessed memory and father-in-law despite the unavoidable intra-family conflicts. I believe all parties contributed to the success of the relationships by showing mutual respect, empathy, understanding, commitment and most of all, love.

Divorce and Separation

Divorce, no matter how imminent and expected, is usually a terrible admission of failure. The sense of loss can be immense; how does one let go of that which they once held so essential? Divorce should be avoided where possible but is sometimes inevitable because of fundamental mistakes in marriage choices. Also, unimaginable and unbearable developments in the marriage experience occur that make differences irreconcilable. Research into the causes of divorce and break-ups of marriage showed five factors as topping the list: strains from parenthood, lack of intimacy, insufficient communication, differing personalities and lack of commitment to the relationship.

New parents can be very surprised by the sheer hard work, sleep deprivation, and other challenges that having young children entails. Being supportive of each other and sharing the responsibilities for home and children is critical especially in early parenting if one party is not to feel overly burdened and disenchanted with the relationship. As the children grow to be adolescents and young adults, parenting challenges might change in nature but the strains can still be felt. You should pay attention to the quality of your relationship if the strain of parenting is not to do irredeemable damage.

By the very nature of sensuality and sexuality, they are not compatible with everyday routines of work and household chores. So how not to lose it by the five-year mark of marriage? The key is to build sensuality in everyday life: a lot of hugs, physical contact, and acts of kindness to surprise. Sensuality helps maintain intimacy, which in turn leads to a sense of belonging and trust.

One of the first victims of cohabiting is explicit communication. Spouses soon learn to 'read' each other rather than talk or listen to each other. This can quickly spiral to loneliness of one party and the longer it goes on, the more difficult it is to rebuild effective communication. When there are issues between couples, it's sometimes considered easier to let things ride instead of stirring up a fight. But the longer couples go without resolving issues, the less engaged in the relationship and the more resentful one or both parties can become. Sometimes, when they finally seek help, the issues might have gone too far and they are not able to find their way back to each other. Once one party lack commitment to the union, it is usually difficult to hold it together.

There is usually a lot of time for both people in a couple to pursue their own passions before marriage such that differing views and personalities might not have been obvious. Once married, these differences might increasingly become important and problematic. The solution? Honour both needs. Create some alone times for each partner. Just two hours a week or a few days a year to enjoy individual interests can help de-stress a marriage. After a three-day holiday with one of my girlfriends, I am usually a calmer participant of the homestead.

Despite the many challenges of matrimony, children are big winners when their parents are able to resolve their differences and abide in marriage. Divorce can be violently shattering for children (at any age, by the way) and its psychological scars can linger well into their own adult life and relationships. It is proven that children, who are spared the horror and heartbreak of a 'broken' home and therefore have a forever notion of their originating family, do prosper by it. The sense of constancy at home leaves children free to concentrate on schoolwork and maintain self-confidence and a sense of security well into adulthood. They should be a major consideration in handling marital crisis and when divorce becomes inescapable, even then it should be navigated with sensitivity about its effects on the children of the marriage.

Conscious Nurture Makes a Successful Marriage

A happy marriage is just like a healthy plant: if you give the plant water, sun, and air, it blossoms. A marriage requires similar nurturing if it is to blossom. No two people are ever totally compatible and are able to have round-the-clock bliss. A long-lasting happy marriage is about knowing your partner and being supportive, kind, and simply nice.

Research shows that for every negative thing you do, you need five positive actions to balance out the effects on your partner. Your marriage can only be happy if the scale is tilted in favour of the positives. Each partner has to be committed to being kind and that is easier done if you are personally fulfilled and find the union satisfying enough to believe in it and want to nurture it. To keep a happy medium, a couple must learn how to identify issues that must be quickly resolved to maintain a positive atmosphere and diffuse tension. You must find and retain your own special way of repairing your relationship when need be. It could be humour, talk, or some action that helps defuse escalating heat, deflect anger, and reset your relationship on an even keel.

Though different people have different ideas about what makes them think their marriage is happy or not, most don't have a definitive content in mind. Certain conditions are however repeatedly ranked high as necessary for a happy marriage. These include respect and attention between partners, mutual emotional support, satisfying intimacy, a sense that the union enhances each partner, and a sense of equity so that problems that might arise are resolvable in a fair manner.

From the perspective of the children, a happy marriage would be the one that provides them with a pleasant family and household atmosphere that support their emotional security. It should endow them with quality parenting that transforms them to well-adjusted adults with joyful childhood memories.

Chapter 8 – Parenting: Not for the Fainthearted

'The thing about parenting rules is that there aren't any. That's what makes it so difficult.'

—Ewan Mcgregor

Children don't ask to be born; adults make that decision, for whatever reasons, which can range from fervently seeking the gift of a child at one end of the spectrum to thoughtlessness at the other. However, if it is that you are a parent or shall be one, be warned: it is a job not for the fainthearted. Not even a high-flying career will prepare you for the constant physical exertion, skill-set, and complexity of emotions and commitment that the task of effective parenting requires. A myriad of people without the understanding of this are parents only in name and let the children grow as weeds, without tending.

Waiting in an airline lounge once, I watched as a parenting nightmare played out right there in public. Mother was all flustered, hoping the close-by audience, myself included, were really concentrating on eating, reading, or watching TV as we appeared to be doing. Father, of course, was totally immersed in work on his laptop while a daughter was 'standing up' to her mother. I was doing all I could not to burst out laughing but wished I could have taken that daughter for a stroll to teach her a few lessons the mother might have left for too late. She, about 18 years old, was inappropriately dressed for family travel in what was really a scanty shimmering cocktail dress, and she was all plied with layers of makeup. She was very loudly talking to someone on her mobile phone plugged into her ears, and Mum was making discreet hand signals for her to lower the volume, I am sure, just for the sake of the rest of us entitled to some peace in the lounge.

Daughter stopped intermittently to grimace at Mother while advancing her noise-making with loud laughs. This went on for about ten minutes until a lounge attendant came to have a word with the 'princess'. And she stopped. Not another sound from her until my flight was called. Mother was now able to relax, seeming relieved that someone else made her daughter behave while Dad continued to be oblivious of the drama that just came to an end.

Really?! What does this tell us about the task? That parenting has to start early; that children will take correction if they respect the source; and beyond all that, that fathers are not excused from their role as parents no matter how important they think their work is!

What Are You Growing Anyway?

In her book *The Blooming Kids*, Joy Haney likens parenting to a gardener's work. In a garden, weeds can grow wildly without cultivation, and they spring up anywhere and everywhere, uninvited and unwanted because they are unsightly.

Roses, on the other hand, rank among the most beautiful flowers but do not just happen; they need to be cultivated. Serious work and consistent care are needed in raising roses, but the resultant beauty is definitely worth all that effort.

The question you should ask yourself as a parent is, "Am I raising beautiful roses, or are weeds sprouting uncontrollably in my home?"

Just as roses are invested in by the grower, your children are in need of even greater investment of your time, love and attention from the moment you set eyes on each other. Training a rosebush is easy when it is still young and malleable, but doing so becomes very difficult if not impossible after it becomes old and gnarled. The same is true with children, conscious parenting should begin at infancy. In your role as a parent, just like in other spheres of life that you need a vision for, you have to decide ahead what kind of children you intend to raise just as a gardener decides what plants would be allowed to dominate the garden – roses or weeds. While all roses do not turn out to be prize roses, an everyday rose is by far more pleasing than a weed, the time spent in nurturing and training a child is never wasted and is a parent's greatest investment with the most amazing rewards of joy and pride.

Parenting a child should be an outstretched hand to love, guide, restrain, or discipline a child. You should consider your parenting role as stewardship to society for the adults that your children would become in future. We all appreciate those outstanding cases of well brought up children and adults that show that someone made the effort to deliberately raise them well, but the evidence of concerted parenting is not apparent from many lives. The only intentions that are constantly mouthed by parents is love for their children and responsibility for picking up the bills for their schooling and upkeep.

As a guide, here are some intentions parents ought to have if they seriously want to succeed at their parenting duties:

- keep the child healthy and nourished for good physical growth;

- train the child to become pleasant and respectful towards others;

- educate the child to ensure his or her potential is optimized to benefit himself or herself and society; and

- protect the children from physical harm and any form of abuse while leading them spiritually.

Even from this short list of intentions, one can already begin to wonder if many parents do in fact pursue such positive intentions. From my observation of many cases it is easy to conclude that there are too few or no intentions at all and that a lot of children are being left to evolve with little or no direction.

Effective parenting should promote and support the physical, emotional, social, spiritual and intellectual development of a child from infancy to adulthood. As a parent, you are expected to impart to them skills, culture, and values until they reach legal adulthood. This is a huge responsibility beyond the biological role of bearing them, and it is for the long haul!

While parenting is one of the most challenging tasks you would ever take on, it also happens to be one of the most rewarding. It demands that you use skills and knowledge that are instinctively learnt, mostly on the job, to give birth, raise, and provide for your child. The task of nourishing and guiding a child requires intense interaction between the parent and the child for a long time beyond childhood. Each child has specific needs and it is by meeting the needs of the child with expressions of love and affection that a positive relationship is built between parent and child.

Parenting Styles and Practices

Parenting is mostly instinctive, but there are some common parenting modes in which most parents raising children can be fitted: authoritative, authoritarian, and permissive. These can be expanded to four to include the uninvolved style. These parenting styles have differing combinations of acceptance and responsiveness on the one hand and demand and control on the other.

Authoritative parenting combines the best balance of demands on the child and responsiveness from the parents. Authoritative parents rely on positive reinforcement and infrequent need to use punishment. Such parents are more attentive and responsive to the child's feelings and capabilities and support the development of the child's personality and potential within reasonable limits. There is good parent-child communication and research has shown that this style is more beneficial than the too-hard authoritarian style or the too-soft permissive style.

Authoritarian parents are very strict and have a rigid set of rules and expectations that require rigid obedience and you will usually find that such parents are not very responsive to the child. Punishment is most often used to ensure future obedience when rules are not obeyed. There is usually no explanation of punishment and "Because I said so" is a typical response to a child's question of authority with little explanation of deeper moral and social implications. Children raised in an authoritarian-style home are moodier, less cheerful, and more vulnerable to stress. In many cases these children may demonstrate passive hostility.

On the other hand, permissive parenting tends to overvalue a child's freedom, and parents become undemanding, so there tends to be little if any explicit rules or punishment. These parents overcompensate by being highly responsive to whatever the child wants at any moment. Children of permissive parents are generally happy but are likely to show low levels of self-control and self-reliance because they would not have learnt those skills due to the lack of structure at home.

An uninvolved or what is actually neglectful parenting style basically results from sheer laziness, with parents in effect absent in their parental role. What occurs here is that there is little or no meaningful communication with the child and such parents are neither responsive to the child's emotional needs nor do they demand much of anything of their children. Children of uninvolved parents tend to be socially incompetent and are likely to exhibit problematic behaviour.

It is sometimes difficult to differentiate between permissive and uninvolved parenting because what is construed as permissive might indeed be lack of involvement. In other words, such parents go through their parenting duties unconsciously. There is nothing worse for the upbringing of a child than a lazy parent: those who are too lazy to provide concerted upbringing, or to admonish and deal with signs of rebellion; too busy to help in a constructive manner; and too lazy to intentionally love with patience and toughness. When a parent is unconscious of a child's changing needs and is not awake enough to recognize the thin line between love and damage, the parent should not be surprised by the consequences of lack of engagement as a parent.

There is no single correct or definitive model of parenting. With the authoritarian and the uninvolved (unconscious) parenting on the opposite ends of the spectrum, most conventional parenting would fall somewhere in between depending on factors like parent's personality and awareness, culture and the particular child. As long as the parent remains awake to duty and applies loving guidance, the child would thrive. There is a reason you are the parent and they, the children. It is because you have been here for longer and should know the way and the pitfalls too. Consider parenting as your stewardship to society and whatever parenting styles and practices you prefer or adopt, parenting success requires skills, patience, and attention. Children benefit immensely from deliberate parenting.

Parenting across the Child's Lifespan

Science has shown that from the fifth month on, the unborn baby is able to hear sounds, become aware of motion, and possibly exhibit short-term memory such that the unborn baby can become familiar with his or her parents' voices. By the seventh month, external schedule cues begin to influence the unborn baby's sleep habits. This is evidence parenting may actually begin well before birth.

Babies

Once the baby arrives, the responsibilities of parenthood become loudly and disruptively obvious. A newborn's basic needs of food, sleep, comfort, and cleaning are obtained through their only form of communication, crying.

Attentive parents will quickly begin to recognize different types of crying for different needs. The insistence of young infants for frequent attention is disruptive to the parents' sleep cycles so that sleep deprivation is the first test of unconditional love for new parents. Bonding at this stage is the foundation of the child's capacity to form and conduct relationships throughout life. Children with secure parental attachment are better able to form successful relationships, express themselves, and have higher self-esteem. Conversely, children who have neglectful caregivers that are emotionally unavailable can go on to exhibit aloofness and defiant behaviour later. So cuddle those babies and give them a sense of security for good bonding!

Toddlers

Toddlers are much more active than infants as they learn how to do simple tasks by themselves and will often mimic their parents. The big challenge for parents at this stage is finding the patience to show the child how to do things rather than just doing things for them. Also, toddlers need help to build their vocabulary, increase their communication skills, and manage their emotions as they should begin to understand social etiquette such as being polite if they are taught. Parents miss this early opportunity because they still consider toddlers babies.

Tantrums begin at this stage, which is sometimes referred to as the terrible twos. Tantrums are either caused by the child's frustration at not being able to communicate properly or for attention seeking, otherwise known as bad behaviour. It is essential at this stage that you help them learn how to handle their frustrations and curtail their tendency to behave with anti- social actions like screaming, hitting or biting others. It is usually not helpful for parents to react to such behaviours with threats and reactive punishments that might only escalate panic on both sides. What is required is taking control in a calm but firm manner.

Young Children

Parenting fun starts at this stage as younger children are more independent and are able to reason and can make their own decisions in simple situations. Young children are good at demanding constant attention, but should be taught how to deal with boredom and play independently with toys and starter books. You can give your children a good start by encouraging social interactions and modelling proper social behaviours by joining them in play. This provides you the opportunity to glimpse into their world, earn their trust, and communicate more effectively with them to offer nurturing guidance. This is when to begin to teach responsibility and consequences of their actions. If you are consistent and fair with discipline, openly offering explanations to your small children, you are likely to encounter fewer problems as they mature. If this stage is absconded by parents and delegated to the maid, nanny, or even preschool teacher, that person becomes the one who sets the rules for the child's actions and behaviours and the one responsible for setting the child's behavioural patterns.

Adolescents

You would often feel frustrated and somewhat isolated in parenting adolescents, but nobody ever promised that job would be easy! It can seem like overnight, and your lovely children have turned into rebellious teenagers! Take many deep breaths and relax; it is the same children testing the freedom that has come with size. It is time to build a deeper relationship with them by taking particular interest in their adolescent activities to gain their trust, in order for them to allow you provide guidance and direction. Adolescence can be a time of high risk for children, where new found freedoms can result in decisions with dire consequences or close off life opportunities.

Although adolescents seem to look to peers and adults outside the family for guidance for how to behave, their parents remain influential in their development. Only the teenager who lacks confidence and positive values follows the crowd. Also, losing interest in schoolwork is usually a result of lacking attention and supervision at home, which further makes them vulnerable to peer pressure. Peer pressure is not the reason peers have influence on your adolescents; they are influenced because they respect, admire, like, and are accepted by those peers!

Your job description at this stage is keeping your promises, not nagging about their past mistakes and trying to listen and 'get' their points of view even if you do not agree. On the other hand, it is the critical time to clearly disapprove of untoward behaviour when they have erred, without alienating the child, so he or she does not turn to the wrong people for acceptance and comfort. Remember to praise your children's strength and celebrate their successes. They are more likely to make the efforts required to get the desired results in future if their efforts are acknowledged. As your child grows through adolescence, always bear in mind how age is affecting the child's behaviour; the same intellectual growth spurt that is making your 13-year-old inquisitive is also responsible for making him or her seem withdrawn or argumentative at the dinner table. It's a thin line to tread with adolescents, but this too shall pass.

Young Adults

The drama can be very different with each young adult even with children of one family with the same upbringing. My baptism of fire was with my first son, who appeared so frustrated with our lack of understanding of his suddenly argumentative stance about any and all matters. Our hitherto civilized household began to experience raised voices and slamming doors over every conversation. I almost turned self-recriminating as I wondered where I could have gone wrong in the 17 or so years leading to this. I became alarmed when my usually 'spoiling parent' husband appeared to be reacting like the stranger in our house could be afflicted with something more sinister than teenage hormones! In the end it took a lot of 'management-style' teaching and encouragement for the young man to focus on the outcomes of his behaviour and learn how to manage us to better achieve the outcomes he sought. This challenging interlude, of course, would be news to close friends and the extended family as they only knew the lovely young boy who then turned a bit quiet and introverted in his late teenage years but has become a most amiable and charming adult.

Then, just when I thought I knew the script and was ready for his younger brother's outbursts, I got none. Relief. That is until the partying years started. Not having fought over curfews and switched off phones (until I heard the key in the lock signifying the dude was home) with the firstborn, I was perplexed. Here was my charming younger son inflicting sleep deprivation and massive doses of worry on us each time he partied. And this went on through senior school and university until his first employers (to whom I will be eternally grateful) wore him out with work and made him, in his own words, an "old man at 21"! All of a sudden he only wanted to catch up with sleep at the weekend, moaning "tired of that scene" when his former party friends tried to get him out.

The volatility that is sometimes exhibited by young adults requires particular attention and understanding by parents. Hopefully, the corrective and character- forming sternness would have been well ministered by a parent during childhood and adolescence such that what is needed to be managed in the young adult is not outright bad manners and wrong values. If that foundational work is not done, it will be an uphill task to try to reason with them at this stage. The crux of the matter is, they are now young adults who believe they know better than the parent, and that is probably true concerning some aspects of their life. They surely know what is going on out there more than you do. What they are likely not to know is that the "mother bird had played in the past the same games and antics as the baby bird is now getting up to" and that the mother bird now has the advantage of hindsight to know how such antics play out. The big challenge you face as the parent of a young adult is how to balance parenting, friendship, and mentoring and how to make them willing to learn from you.

Navigating the transition from your parental control mode during their childhood and adolescence to becoming the parent that can be trusted and respected enough to be looked up to for advice and as role model is very tricky. Conflicts between young adults and their parents result from communication failure and disrespect can arise when a young person is not proud of or impressed by what the parent represents. This is a bitter pill for a parent to swallow but it is what it is. Parents have to work on being the parent that can keep their children's youthful pride and temperament in check. Young adults can be most critical and seemingly unkind. They have not been humbled by life experiences, making them arrogant in their outlook and judgment of others, especially their parents.

As a parent of young adults, you need to learn to understand their confusion, anxiety, struggles, and individuality. While you wish to guide them from your own life experience and loving concern for them, you should be more considerate of their stage of life and what is best for them. Your job is to help the child be the best he or she can be not insist your child becomes what you want.

Adults

You don't suddenly stop being a parent when your child becomes a mature adult. Support and counsel continue to be needed in your child's life for all times. Ultimately, each child becomes an adult that would sometimes make choices very different from the parent's opinion or advice. At this stage it makes for good order that your parenting role is to engage in gentle guidance and discussions with healthy respect for the views of the adult your child has become.

As parents age and their children have their own families, continuing good relationship and friendship is beneficial to both sides and some role reversal in some aspects become noticeable if the relationship remains healthy and is extended to their spouses and the grandchildren.

Parenting is a lifelong engagement. As is said, the work of the parent is never done. I still get food packs from my mum, and I am heading for 60!

Parenting Special Needs Children

The very obvious special needs cases can usually not be ignored and are firmly dealt with. A higher level of mindfulness is required for the borderline cases as diagnoses and management are often confusing. The level and type of support needed and for how long in each case can be diverse. Be it academic, emotional, or physical, appropriateness and promptness of help are critical, depending on correct or independent diagnoses of the exact malfunction and the level of functionality that can be achieved by the child. Planning for adulthood of special needs children should be dealt with openly to afford them dignity and a good level of normalcy.

Parental Role in the Adults We become: Enabling Your Child

The parenting you give your children has a far-reaching effect on the kind of adults they become. You can help in making them possess the kind of savvy that allows them to get the best from the world and achieve their potential. While this savvy can be learnt or developed later in life, being given it from youth gives one a better go at life right from the starting block.

According to sociologist Annette Lareau, there are only two parenting philosophies, and they divide almost perfectly along class lines. The wealthier middle-class parenting philosophy is 'concerted cultivation', where a parent attempts to actively nurture and access a child's talents, skills, and opportunities. Poorer parents, by contrast, and usually not by choice, tend to follow a strategy of 'accomplishment of natural growth'. This group see their responsibility for caring for their children but not their role in improving their potentials, mainly because they lack both the understanding and opportunities for concerted cultivation.

While one style is not morally better than the other, concerted cultivation has enormous advantages as it confers to the children some sense of entitlement in the most positive connotation of the word. The child that has been so cultivated is better off not only because he or she goes to a better school and has more privileges but also because, and perhaps this is even more critical, the sense of entitlement or importance he or she has been taught is an attitude perfectly suited to succeeding in the modern world.

Of course there are exceptions. My father was one parent that practiced concerted cultivation and could not be said to be wealthy when I was raised. You can envision and cultivate your child for success and make concerted effort to seek out opportunities that would differentiate them from the herd, even when you are borderline middle class and have not attained wealth.

Envisioning Your Child

'Where there is no vision the people perish.'

—Proverbs 29: 18

It is a shame but true that what gifted children from lower social and economic classes (and indeed some with well-off parents that are too uninvolved to envision their children despite being socially and economically able) lack for achieving their potential is not something expensive or difficult to find; nor is it encoded in DNA. What they lack could actually have been given to them by the community around them. The children who grow up without this gift of cultivation and envisioning can become squandered talent. As a parent, you should see your responsibility to lead and help your children to a future of self-actualisation and confidence by guiding, teaching, sharing experience, encouraging, pointing out signposts, and seeking opportunities without becoming overbearing and controlling. If you ponder your role and contribution to the success of your children as adults in the not–so-distant future, you might be able to harness the energy and attention required to make them the kind of successors you would like to see, not only or necessarily in financial terms but more importantly in terms of self-actualisation, culture, and values.

Cheerleading is Your Role

Every child, no matter how bright and intelligent, can do with and is definitely further motivated by an audience to bounce for. The first sign of this need shows up when a toddler waves with pride and shouts out, "Mummy, Daddy, see!" when he has stacked his colour bricks right or managed to climb the frame in the playground to the top.

This need to be applauded continues in a child, albeit significantly hidden and not as openly demanded as they mature. It is there and, I believe, always there, even into the adult years. It is only lost if there is no active audience participation and this is easily picked up by the child. The error is that parents stop cheering when it's no longer openly demanded; I believe I still bounced for my father's approval right to the end of his life, and I was in my forties. I know our own adult sons love to surprise us with their achievement news. It is also telling to note how most speeches by recipients of success awards are chockfull of messages to and about parents who cheered on their way up there.

The cheerleading audience for a child is not always or necessarily a biological parent; as long as the child respects and desires the good opinion of a person and therefore would strive to impress them, that person should actively be a cheerleader.

Your Sacrifice at Critical Moments

There are defining moments in raising each child when a parent has a choice to make between creating the required time or resources to support the child if he or she were to optimise his or her potential or not. These moments present themselves as crisis or nuisance moments and a lack of attention by parents can make the opportunities in them lost.

My most vivid recollection of compromise was in 1990 when I elected to reduce my hours by a third in my consulting job at the time. It had become apparent that my older son, then 6 years old, was absolutely unhappy about the after-school arrangement we had with a neighbouring family with children in the same school. His regular outbursts about his exclusion from activities being the only outsider among the five or six siblings of the house became increasingly heartbreaking as I dropped him off at school every morning, especially as the school itself was particularly family-oriented. Parents were included in school excursions and extracurricular activities and other parents would give me snippets of how my son excelled at such activities as I hurriedly dropped him off before heading to work. I finally braved a meeting with my group senior manager and asked to reduce my work hours to allow me be there at the school gate and have enjoyable afternoons with my son. Peter, the group manager, my friend to this day, miraculously accepted! A miracle as I had only recently been promoted manager with client responsibilities. I remain grateful to Peter for making it easy for me to work part-time when it was necessary for my son's wellbeing. That period allowed me to participate in after school activities like tea with other families, develop friendship with the mothers of his friends, and most importantly my child was euphorically happy to have his mum at the school gate too!

Teaching Your Child How to Relate to Money

A grounded sense of value and a saving culture should start with the piggy bank. Refusing to be your children's automatic cash dispenser is teaching them delayed gratification and prioritizing in spending because children can quickly become prone to impulsive spending. Teach them by your actions and talk how to differentiate between want and need. Encourage them to take holiday jobs to inculcate the pride of own earnings as well as spending discipline for a healthy financial future. You can encourage a saving culture through bonus incentives on whatever a child saves. Whatever be the case, it is advised that teaching children about the value of money should start as early as possible.

If a healthy value and respect of money has not been effectively imbibed, succession planning will become a challenge where there is an inheritance to pass on. If you have failed in teaching them responsible management and ownership of money, it is most unlikely for such inheritance to be grown or passed on beyond their own generation.

Discipline is Critical

Jo Frost, better known as *Super Nanny* because of her twenty-five years' experience in helping troubled families, suggests many parents are afraid to discipline, sometimes because they feel guilty that they work and don't spend the desirable amount of time they wish they could with their children. They end up saying yes to everything and don't learn to say no, just to make them feel better about their guilt. Oftentimes parents proffer the excuse of their own scarred childhood and then overcompensate in the area of discipline regarding their own children. To discipline, however, is part of being a responsible parent.

The evidence we see of a spoilt child is never the result of showing a child too much love. It is usually the consequence of absence of discipline and giving a child things in place of love, things like undue leniency, lowered expectations, or material possessions. Discipline has to begin very early. If you do not manage your child's behaviour when he is young, he will have a hard time learning self-control when older. Well-explained rules have to be set and established regarding behaviour and limits. Mindful parents would have expectations they want their child to live up to, hence the rules. Talking about explained rules, parents tend to over-explain to young children who cannot comprehend the explanations and under-explain to adolescents who require them!

While it is good to foster your children's independence to help them develop a sense of self direction, setting limits within that freedom helps your child develop a sense of self-control. To be successful in life, they are going to need both. It is normal human reaction for children to resist control, push for autonomy and test the boundaries. Consistency is the critical success factor in discipline. If your rules vary from day to day in an unpredictable fashion or if you enforce them only intermittently, it could lead to rebellion. Once you make clear your nonnegotiables, please remain consistent. The more your authority is based on unchanging wisdom and not on power play depending on the situation, the less your child will challenge it.

Harsh discipline should be avoided as much as possible despite the 'spare the rod, spoil the child' school of thought. Children who are spanked or slapped have been found to be more prone to fighting with other children and are more likely to be bullies that use aggression to solve disputes with others.

There are many other ways to discipline a child beyond the cane. Some favourite that I have found effective are time outs, curfew, or withholding of objects or privileges.

Teaching Your Child Responsibility as Early as Possible

Most of the values you would want your child to portray all hinge on responsibility. If a child is able to display responsible social behaviour, he or she is bound to be successful in handling most aspects of life. Your main goal of teaching responsibility is for children to learn self-control and to feel responsibility for the outcomes of their own behaviour. It is not enough to teach your children manners or respect if they do not possess a sense of responsibility for their action and its effect on themselves and others. Responsibility is one of if not the most important element of good character that children need in order to prepare them for adult life.

As soon as children are old enough to comprehend it, they should be held responsible for tasks and the effects of their behaviour and actions well discussed and analysed. They should also be made to accept responsibility for the outcome of their action rather than seek excuses or shift blame to everybody else. Do not wait until your child is older before instilling responsibility as the effort required later to change formed irresponsible habits is painful and frustrating for parent and child.

Motherhood and Fatherhood

'The good child is the father's child but the bad is the mother's.'

—A Yoruba saying

The antecedents of this saying and its proper context was to motivate the indigenous women in polygamous situations, where each mother nurtured her own biological children to be deliberate in raising good children that the father and the community would be proud of. The ideology of motherhood portrays mothers as being the ultimate caregivers because they invest a significant amount of time on their children to nurture them and support their emotional growth and stability usually at the expense of other aspects like work and career.

Whereas in the past, fathers were solely the breadwinners and the mothers stayed at home to take care of children, but roles are starting to converge. Fathers now more than ever are spending more time with their children and participating more and taking on responsibilities in parenting roles. In her book *Strong Fathers, Strong Daughters*, Meg Meeker emphasizes the importance of fathers' roles in shaping who their daughters become. She claims, "Fathers, more than anyone else, set the course for a daughter's life".

I can personally testify to that from my experience and would encourage fathers to take more than a fleeting interest in their children's lives from an early stage, daughters and sons alike. Fathers should not seek to ascribe the blame for a problematic child (bad child) to only the mother. Both parents are responsible for the adults that all their children become, hopefully all good.

What You Do and Say Matter So Much

Parents run the risk of unknowingly impacting and sometimes damaging their children through their words, actions, or inactions. Talking in the presence of your children about matters that should never be exposed to them can have long lasting or permanent effects on them. Children imitate parents and other adults they are exposed to. What you say and do matter, be it your personal habits or the way you treat other people; your children are learning from you all the time. You should especially be mindful not to react to situations in the spur of the moment in the presence of children. Remain conscious of the lessons being learnt by the children present from your situations and discussions. Venting about other people, including your spouse and extended family without the sensitivity of the effects on the children present is a common pitfall. Making snide comments about other adults is teaching the children disrespect for those adults and yourself as their view of adults in general is being diminished making them lose the natural elevated opinion of adults. Also, if your actions lack compassion and courtesy to other people, your children are likely to grow up lacking those attributes as they have not had the opportunity to learn them from you.

Not Too Much Protection or Assistance—Free Them to Fly

The harm caused by this parenting error is best portrayed by the example of the mother butterfly and the baby moth. The baby moth arrives in a cocoon from which it needs to free itself by hitting its growing wings against its inside until the cocoon breaks open. This exercise is meant to strengthen the moth's wings and prepare it for flying as a butterfly. Apparently, any help by the mother butterfly in breaking open the cocoon results in the baby butterfly being freed before its wings have been strengthened enough by its own struggle to break the cocoon. Its inability to fly with undeveloped wings ultimately results in its destruction, as it is unable to fly to safety when necessary.

Parents agonize over the delicate balance between withholding from their children enough to make them strong, understand value, and become able to strive for their own prosperity on one hand, and lovingly meeting their children's' whims, no matter how unreasonable or premature, on the other hand. When parents satisfy the requests of their children and give them a soft lifestyle too early, those children can quickly lose any sense of value and indeed of perspective. It is most unfortunate and pitiful to watch as such youngsters are likely to become adults with an insatiable appetite for luxury matched with a lack of enthusiasm for valuable work. Many young adults give laughable excuses like the lack of challenge, excitement, or passion as reasons for not staying in jobs, including family businesses.. Their parents in such situations are usually faced with no option but to play along as the character traits have been set and their baby moth simply can't fly.

And Then the Empty Nest

You will be tempted at the height of active parenting to dream of the day when you and your spouse can have the peace of your household back. When the endless swimming lessons, football trips, ballet classes, and extra French classes have you in a merry-go-round daze. The temptation becomes a veritable prayer when the teenage years further try your usually loving parental patience, and if anyone listened closely, they can hear you muttering under your breath, "When, O Lord?"

I will advise that you observe the empty-nesters around you and if you get a chance to talk to them about your hope for a quiet and orderly homestead, you might hear them recall the "sweet old days of active parenting". That should tell you a thing or two about enjoying your children and that joyously busy time while it lasts! Because all of a sudden, all those plans for boarding school and university begin to materialize, and the home presence of each child begins to dwindle. First you have him or her for Easter, summer, and Christmas; then it becomes just summer and Christmas if there are no summer programs that keep the child away. And then, without warning, its just work leave at Christmas. Two weeks if you're lucky!

The eight-year gap between my children stretched out the time before I finally got to the stage of full nest only at Christmas. No matter how much work or activities you fill your time with, it is simply never a satisfying diversion if you were a hands-on parent. But that is exactly what you need to do, get a life! Get busy with fulfilling and enjoyable work and activities. An empty nest should be planned for ahead as one does for retirement if the suddenness of it is not to lead to a kind of sadness from a sense of no longer being needed.

Endeavour to Grow Prize Roses!

Anyone who has been mildly successful in parenting knows that raising children to be prize roses in not an easy task. You will struggle from time to time with the seeming endlessness of the responsibility. Things do get better after the pandemonium of looking after young children, and you should remember to enjoy the ride, albeit a bumpy one, at every stage. Of those active parenting years are fond memories made and good relationships with your children built. The family ties resulting from those years will determine to a large extent the quality of your family life over the next four or five decades, long after they have left home... but they never really leave if the ties are good and strong.

Parenting is one of the aspects of life where you must endeavour to guide deliberately to purpose, as you help your children turn ambivalence into enthusiasm, laziness into diligence, self-doubt to confidence – the list is long! Be committed to consciously helping your children become prize roses who forge ahead and accomplish great things, not just weeds left alone in the struggle of life. That is why you preceded them, and that is why you are the parent.

Chapter 9 - When Life Happens

'If we were not prepared to meet the temptations that we are to undergo, we would open the door to a great enemy – discouragement and gloominess.'

—Francis Fernandez

Life sometimes happens – in different dimensions and intensity, and mostly when it is least expected. If you are wise, you would know by now that some matters, usually destabilising, are out of your control.

Whatever the reason for a destabilising occurrence, the most important thing is that you consciously look for that purpose so the experience is not wasted in undue grief or struggle. In seeking the purpose, you allow the experience to achieve what it is purposed to do.

If discouragement and gloominess result from being ill-prepared to meet the temptations and challenges of life, the burning question is how then can one be better prepared and still live life with optimism? In as much as it is impossible to be always prepared for traumatic occurrences in life, the strengthening of character and resilience to be gained from living to a consciously adopted philosophy for one's life is a good preparation that can forestall the enemy of absolute gloom when life happens. Self-knowledge and compassion built beforehand also help to consciously and adequately manage reactions when life throws a curve. In other words, a peaceful and well-centred life would be more prepared to absorb shocks than an already cacophonous state of existence.

My Own Baptism of Fire

'There are no mistakes, only lessons to be learnt. There is a purpose for everything that has ever happened to you and everything that will happen to you. Every experience offers lessons.'

—Robin Sharma, *The Monk Who Sold his Ferrari*

My own experience supports the monk's take that everything happens for a reason. The reason can be causal, the effect of past causes or a significant signpost on a life journey that redirects it. When life happens and stops you in your tracks, seeking your full attention whether you like it or not, there is usually some purpose to it. It could be the orchestration to stop you from continuing on a route that is not the best for you and force a rerouting; it could be to release or force you to go and be more, to do things you ought to be doing before it becomes too late. Whether that purpose is ultimately served depends solely on how you perceive and handle the situation and the level of fortitude and self-knowledge that you have built up before then.

One of the interview questions that still intrigue me is the one that asks the candidate to tell where he or she expects to be in five years. As a member of panels at interviews, I would usually listen to many candidates rustle up some likely plan while they appear not to believe their own story. Once in a while, however, some candidate seems very articulate and sure of the plan and goals they aspire to in five years, their confidence of getting there palpable. I have wondered if anyone interviewing me was ever so convinced that I had a plan that I so believed in ... but I always had a vision of the specific places I was headed in terms of career and family. I describe my journey to the professional success (at least so it seemed to me) that I had achieved by

2002 as a backdrop and to give a sneak view to how I felt when life happened then and how difficult my journey to recovery was.

My career, despite many moves for family reasons, was one of the aspects of life that I was passionate about, albeit in a private manner. I had aspirations for which I tried to plan. I say I tried to plan because family life meant necessary flexibility in such plans.

My most pivotal career plan was hatched in 1990 while I was a consulting manager in the London office of KPMG. I had become aware of the significant change and growth in the banking sector in my home country, Nigeria, in the late 1980s, and I began to think of my career prospects for when my family moved back to Nigeria, as we planned to do in a couple of years, and felt that banking would be the way to go. So it was that I approached the banking group in the firm with the request to move over from the business services group; I got lucky and was moved to the banking group.

I consulted to banking clients in the next two years and gained some useful experience that would be useful for joining a bank without being a total novice. When my family relocated to Lagos in December 1992, the job search led me to a position heading strategic planning and internal audit in one of the banks. I was reluctant to accept the job because I wanted to practice banking, not be boxed into an audit job.

The Managing director of the bank and I arrived at a compromise: I would set up the internal audit department and train my replacement before I could move into mainstream banking in two years. That arrangement worked perfectly for my career evolution. As strategic planner, auditor, and member of the executive committee, I combined work with training and was ready in two years when I was appointed head of treasury and special credits. I learnt more banking skills in the next three years and began to receive work offers from other banks for mainstream banking positions. It was time to set further career goals for the future.

Having scanned the industry and consulted widely, and despite better offers from other banks, I accepted an offer from the foremost banking brand in the country. That move was based on my belief that concluding my career at the directorate level of the bank would be a fulfilling one. I threw myself into making a mark, and my hard work was recognised and rewarded. I was promoted within two years of joining and became a visible member of top management. Things were working out as hoped and planned – until life happened. Big time!

With loud publicity, a very significant credit granted by the bank for the acquisition of a public asset fell through, and the bank lost the non-refundable deposit paid on behalf of a borrower for the acquisition because the credit had not been structured to include the appropriate security for the bank to compensate itself. The board fired both the managing director and the executive director responsible for the credit. At the time I sympathised with the two because I believed they might only have been too enthusiastic for the bank to be at the forefront of a large ticket transaction. As treasurer I was not a member of the credit committee of the bank; I only had credit responsibilities for funds invested with other banks, and despite the turbulence in the money market at the time, not one of those placements was lost by the bank. For good control, the treasury department could not transfer funds out of the bank, not even for bank placements initiated by treasury. All physical fund movements were the responsibility of the operations department that was in another directorate.

The credit funding request for the failed transaction had been sent to the bank's treasury four months earlier by the managing director of the bank with his approving signature appended. As treasurer, I noted payment was to the government body collecting for the asset being acquired and stated the funding source on same document (request), and passed it to the head of operations, who was of the same seniority as myself. In this case the head of operations sent a confirmation of settlement to the managing director to confirm the payment was indeed made before the deadline. It was therefore a surreal experience when a disciplinary committee was constituted after the exit of the two directors, to which a few officials including myself were invited to face. I explained that I did not make a credit decision, nor did I make a fund transfer. The committee's opinion implied that I could have truncated a funds transfer request for a credit of the bank that the managing director had approved; also that the head of operations carried out the transfer only because I so 'instructed'. So it was that the operations officials that transferred the funds based on the request of the managing director were found faultless.

I was shocked and furious in equal measures at what was obviously a hunt for a scapegoat! When it became apparent that my career at the bank might be plagued by these developments, I decided to resign. My letter to that effect was duly acknowledged, but the powers that be would have none of that! I received a termination letter from the bank four days after 1 had resigned. I sought legal opinion and decided to seek justice. So it was that I sued the largest bank in the country at that time, asking for no money compensation, only to clear my name. My prayers to the court was to prove that 1 was not guilty of either negligence or misconduct and that as I had resigned, my resignation should be accepted by the bank unless they found me culpable in some way. It took nine years in the slow justice system of Nigeria, but by 2011 judgment was finally delivered in my favour. The bank has withdrawn its termination letter, accepted my resignation, and corrected my records.

My Path to Survival

How I survived the initial sadness for the malicious harm done to my carefully planned and nurtured career by that occurrence in 2002, I still try not to dwell upon. But I found a reservoir of strength and resilience I did not know 1 could muster. It was indeed a time of despair and anger, but I was fortunate to quickly realise I could not afford the luxury of letting despair overwhelm and dictate my reactions if I were to survive what appeared to be a career calamity. I acknowledged my right to anger at what I considered the unfairness and persecution by the bank, I was able to separate the uncontrollable events from what I could control and took steps to heal by immersing myself initially in healing activities like travelling, reading, and generally being with family and close friends.

I allowed my anger to propel me to be brave, focussed, and insistent in what I needed to do; I fought back, became creative, and ultimately flourished. Instituting a court case was my fight back; it made me feel less of a hopeless victim; in the nine years it took to obtain a vindicating judgment, I believe despair was kept at bay because I was stubbornly fighting back despite the common sentiment by many that I could not take on the elephant. Creativity and deliberateness were born of the need to get back to the drawing board to chart a new course for myself. I took my own usual advice to other people to recognise the purpose in the chaos to redirect my work and life. In rethinking the future, I recalled my growing dissatisfaction with my work-life balance in the couple of years before this time. I knew I was dropping some balls in my parenting role but still felt lucky to have my career. This was an opportunity to correct things.

The result of all that reflection was that I decided, in the face of tempting job offers, to start creating my own made-for-purpose line of work that would make me more attentive to my family while creating financial value through fulfilling work to adequately meet the lifestyle I desired. I was finally able to sincerely review the possibilities of work that would use my training, natural talents and passion for a fulfilling balance.

Less than a year later I became less agitated by my experience at First Bank and developed the presence of mind to dwell further on my dreams; dreams that were forming during the previous few years but for which I might not have voluntarily left the job. Real estate development and investments was where I pitched my tent. I started a real estate investment business from our small home office. The first project was a twenty-five unit office park spanning two thousand square metres on three floors. My hitherto membership of the banking industry served me well in terms of contacts for raising funding for the project, and I was no stranger to the cash-flow dynamics of small commercial real estate projects. I had previously developed an interest in building project management through working with different contractors as we built our own homes. However, the fact that I fought the case to obtain judgement against the bank and had my records restituted meant that when the opportunity to serve as a non-executive director of a Pan African bank came, I was able to take it. The rest is history, – a very good history.

Also, opportunity and freedom to pay the necessary attention to nurture my sons on their way to adulthood, while building the business for a more valuable future, is beyond any doubt a great purpose in all that mayhem. I am grateful and fulfilled that I flourish despite that setback in 2002 and fourteen years later I cannot imagine another path that would have led me to my present fulfilment. I thrived while riding the storm, as long and tough as it was, without succumbing hopelessly to the waves.

Trauma Effect... You Need a Paradigm Shift

'Life's challenges are not supposed to paralyse you, they are supposed to help you discover who you are.'

—Bernice Johnson Reagon

When any kind of deep loss or negativity occurs in life, such as loss of material possession, a close relationship, personal reputation, a job or physical ability, something on the inside is immediately diminished because of the loss of control and resulting helplessness. This can in turn affect your sense of who you are, a form of disorientation; without that which has been lost, be it a job, a relationship, or possession, a person might ask of themselves, "Who am I without this job, this possession, or this relationship?"

The loss of the identity that you had unconsciously assumed can be extremely painful and leave a hole, so to speak, in the fabric of your existence. When this happens, as it would, the needed healing demands that you do not deny or ignore the pain or sadness that is felt. It is in fact all important that this acceptance takes place to neutralise the mind's tendency to panic and construct a fearful story around that loss in which you are assigned the role of hopeless victim in free fall. Fear, anger, resentment, long-term anxiety, and sometimes self-pity are the emotions that go with that role of victim; hopelessness for the future is fearful to everyone. If you are able to acknowledge what lies behind those emotions and question their rationale, you may find it is no longer such a fearful place. You may be surprised to find acceptance and peace, even some confidence from being able to question the validity of those fears and emptiness!

It is from this place of acceptance and the peace following that you are able to see the new opportunities and directions that would fill the hole and ease the pain. There is a potential for redemption in every crisis, but only if you allow yourself to reach that place of freedom from fear and become aware of the potential. If you allow yourself that required paradigm shift.

Often, at the height of dealing with a negative drama, the tendency is to seek relief by hoping that all will return to the former state. It is however important to realize that all dramas have multiple possibilities and opportunities that may be different from the past or your construed expectation of the future. It is ultimately your choice to consciously review all the possibilities in order to react appropriately for you to choose your best route or opportunity. It is common that choice at such moments is made difficult if not impossible because of the pain and all the other players involved. This is why it is advisable to stay still for some moment when life happens to clear your head and make the paradigm shift required to bring you back in control of your thoughts to consider all the probable outcomes that are available before choosing the path you might best pursue.

Getting Back on the Boat—Regaining Control

After the moment taken to still yourself after a traumatic experience, you should be fully awake to the fact that, while it would be difficult, you need to climb back into the boat of your life and start paddling again. The sheer effort to do this is usually difficult to summon immediately but you must bear in mind that you cannot hide away for ever and would have to pick up the paddles again if you were to recover. It is the only way to take back control after the helplessness you might have experienced. Recovery entails looking at the possibilities ahead to find your path. Often, you might have to move through not so ideal circumstances to get to the right place, this is made more difficult because of the emotional state you are likely to be in. So when life happens, consider that it may be a difficult step in the right direction and summon the courage to accept those tough times as you would embrace the easy ones. Knowing and accepting that it is a journey of continual growth would help keep you focussed and motivate you to make the required effort.

When Life Happened: Some of My Heroes

'The abundant life does not come to those who have had a lot of obstacles removed from their path by others. It develops from within and is rooted in strong mental and moral fibre.'

—William Lewis

I have been humbled as I have observed at close range how some brave people have brought to bear very strong mental fibre to liberate themselves when they were taken by unpleasant surprise as life took some unexpected turns. From my close observation I marvel at their bravery and refusal to drown in despair and self-pity. I tell their stories below. I also survived my own baptism of fire, not because I knew the rules to apply but because the required strength, which even I did not know existed, showed up when needed. Sometimes the rules get made along the way, fit for purpose, but only if you had developed a strong mental strength hitherto and remain open to possibilities when life happens. You can enjoy an abundant life despite unexpected obstacles, but you should endeavour to prepare yourself mentally and morally to beat down those obstacles when they rear their heads.

My Mother Survives

In my search for heroes, an unlikely candidate that I have seen at close quarters all my life suddenly crept into mind: my own mother. This epiphany occurred when I decided a few years ago to surprise her at her church on her birthday, which fell on a Sunday that year. As I drove there, I called my cousin who attends the same church to ensure I was not going to be the one in for a surprise if my mother had decided to fellowship at some other Baptist congregation on that day. He assured me he knew she was billed to render a song with the choir during service to mark her birthday.

It suddenly got me thinking about her and how quite independent she had become since life happened to her about twenty-six years earlier. Almost thirty years ago, I received a call from my mother that she had just been served with summons for divorce proceedings brought by my dad. My wonderful father (and my father was truly special in many ways) might have succumbed to the middle-age crisis pitfall of wanting to experience life in a more dramatic way, or maybe the unhappy state of their marriage had become unbearable to him. My mother, like all humans, had her own faults. Whatever the fault lines, the shock and sadness that washed over me as she told me the news is indescribable even now. My web of emotions and thoughts at that point was the culmination of the pain and insecurity of living through my parents' fragile marriage; and just when I thought we had hacked it and they had managed to keep it all together, despite the fact that my Muslim dad had recently taken a much younger wife, then this!

With these thoughts came a wave of sadness because of the injustice that I believed and still believe had been done to my mother. While my mum is no saint, she had sown her life from the early age of 18 to tend to our family. She'd had to grow up fast, dropping the mantle of childhood and student to pick up that of mother and wife. She had cooked, cleaned, washed, moved our family from one home to another from town to town, and had gone to paid employment when money was sparse. Granted, there was not much warmth at home in the few years preceding this event, it was important to me, as it is to any child, that our family was intact. It was still important to me that my mother lived at home to give me some semblance of a family life despite my being married and gone.

How she emotionally bore those last few years in the polygamous setting, I still cannot surmise or dwell upon. But she stayed. Apparently, even that existence was no longer acceptable and she had to leave. At that point my mother had no property or much money to her name but still held her secretarial job at one of the public sector ministries. So ended the only life she had known all her adult life. Their marriage was dissolved after a few hearings without any settlement deserving of mention. The swiftness and lack of reasonable settlement might have been because theirs was an Islamic marriage or that she could not afford legal representation.

Between hearing the news and the dissolution, I went to meet with my father to try to reason with him. I can't now remember his exact words, but his message was tantamount to "the die is cast". The outcome of that meeting chipped away a significant chunk of my confidence in humankind because my trust up to then in other people was predicated on my trust of my father's compassionate and fair nature.

My mother's journey from then until now is a study in survival. She soldiered on in her job. Her employers granted her a mortgage and sold her a house priced for the management cadre once I signed up to a monthly contribution because she could not really afford it on her secretary salary. I had just qualified and had a good starter job, so I could.

When I think of the life she has carved out for herself in her neighbourhood and especially the local Baptist church congregation, I see a hero that has endured years of hardship, unfairness, and humiliation but never succumbed to hopelessness. I can't imagine the thoughts that must have kept her awake in those earlier days when the wound was fresh with the sheer embarrassment of feeling discarded. Now I do the sums and realise that she was only 48 years old at the time of the separation, I am even more amazed at how a life could have been so destabilised at 48 but still thrive.

I watched on that day as she filed in with the choir into church in her choir robe, and I could not but be proud. As I watched, I wondered why it took me until then to appreciate her strength, bravery, and survival virtues. It could not have been easy, but she soldiers on.

Pamela, My Friend and Sister, Humbles Me

Another person whose experience has humbled me is Pamela. I met her at postgraduate accommodation in London thirty-six years ago. Although we were in different disciplines, she law and me accountancy, we somehow found each other and became a sisterhood. We found our early childhood history to be very similar, born to very young mothers and spent early years with maternal grandmothers in similar settings in West Africa, she in Sierra Leone, I in Nigeria. I believe our affinity and ease of communication stem from that grandmotherly influence, and somehow the impact of those early years still resonates with both of us deeply even now. Our relationship could not be better if we were blood sisters. Despite very different life paths in the past thirty-six years, we still totally get each other, and no matter how long since the last meeting or catch up, there is absolutely no gap in our conversation.

Pamela's life focus and pride was her legal career in the public sector in the UK, where she had been well recognized for her commitment. By 2005, she was heading the legal team of the mayoralty of London. In July of that year, she experienced another elating professional moment when London won the bid to be the Olympic city and had just flown back to London on the seventh of July 2005 after the result was announced at the selection ceremony in Europe the previous day. She got into the underground train system at Kings Cross station of London to go home briefly before heading for work. Then, what is commonly referred to today as the 7/7 terrorist blast, happened at that station.

Pamela, in her own recollection of the mayhem, woke up in the wreckage, not feeling much pain but hearing people moaning for help as she recognized that the person lying next to her was dead. She also noticed one of her own legs at what appeared to be a strange angle to her body. She recalls being very weak and falling in and out of consciousness. She says that in those fleeting moments before help arrived, she thought about dying and how it was the thought of her family that propelled her to hang in there and live.

I was in Minneapolis in the States when the news of the blast flashed over the television, and I had contacted my older son who had just written his final examination at university and was in London awaiting his degree to confirm his safety. Then I got an email from Pamela's husband that she had been injured in the blast, giving me details of the hospital where they had taken her. I called my son again to inform him and gave him details of how to find her at the hospital. He found her but could not report to me that she had lost one of her legs in the blast. I only found out through a follow-up email from Pamela's husband.

It has been seventeen years as I write this, during when I thought I understood what she had gone through since the occurrence. But I had not until we spent three days together in Greece in July 2014, exactly nine years to the blast, and we finally had the time and freedom to have a no-holds-barred talk about that fateful day and her journey since. I finally gleaned some idea of her torturous journey to date. As she told me about her physical, emotional, and psychological journey of nine years I realised that I had not really travelled that road with her for the simple reason that we live in different countries. I heard about how she had come to terms with the physical activities which she can no longer participate in; the details of the forward planning that have become normal to her just to care for her family and go to work on a daily basis; the frequent trips to the limb centre and how she has to manage her expectation to avoid upsets and irritation when those visits become necessary. I did not know before then the number of further surgeries she had had to endure after the initial amputation. When we went on to the matter of occasional low moods, I was mortified as I remembered how she had counselled me just the day before to snap out of the unhappiness and frustration I was experiencing regarding the administration of my late father's estate. I marvelled at how bubbly she had been during that holiday despite all that. We discussed for the first time how this had affected her cherished career and family life, and I heard how their lovely home had had to be extensively reengineered to allow her be as independent as possible.

I believe that during the nine-year anniversary, the much-publicized remembrance of the event in which she granted media interviews and spoke openly and confidently of her experience immensely advanced her emotional recovery. She confirmed that she finally found a refreshed joy for life. We agreed during those three days to consciously live joyfully and decided to have an annual get away, just the two of us. When I think of her and the challenges she has navigated, and still does, I am humbled and respectful. I am also very proud of the progress she has made in her career and public service space up to date.

Tola Makes Me Proud to Be Her Friend

I met Tola just a couple of years ago in the most unlikely way for finding a soul mate. I had gone in my line of duty to make enquiries about an interesting real estate development in the centre of my city when I was ushered into the presence of the most pleasant executive I have ever encountered in a government establishment. I went ready for the difficulty and information-hoarding stance common with office holders in the public sector and I kept pinching myself during that meeting if she could be real. Without my having been referred to her by a known person, she was surprisingly helpful, open and friendly, explaining the project timelines and details and she promised to place me on the waiting list and keep me informed.

And informed she has kept me. As I write, the project is yet to be completed or allocated, but we've become tight buddies. We now meet for meals and drinks once in a while, sharing life experiences and challenges. I am particularly honoured that in one of our evenings, she shared her bumpy road to motherhood, and I would never have imagined such a challenging journey, going by her cheerful mien, warmth, and childlike enthusiasm.

Tola had been married to her equally wonderful husband for about thirty years when she shared her story. In her late fifties, she had been through all the fertility treatment routes you can think of but had not been able to biologically mother a baby. She had adopted her first daughter about ten years earlier. Considering the burden of infertility in the African cultural setting where procreation can be made to seem like the reason for being, hers must have been a tough decision to have navigated and accepted.

Almost a year into our friendship I got a curious message from Tola about an event that had required her to be off work for some time. She promised she would explain when we met next. A thousand quick thoughts came to my mind; could she have become pregnant at 56 and be on bed rest? Could she be suffering from an ailment? I was perplexed but decided to play it cool and write her a text appreciating her trust in sharing the situation with me and that I awaited the time to talk. True to her word, about a month later, she summoned me to a café one evening and shared ...

Apparently, Tola, in all those challenging years, deeply believed it would be more satisfying for her family if they had a child sired by her husband even though she could not incubate that child herself. So, headstrong woman that she is, she researched surrogacy arrangements and convinced her husband to cooperate to sire his child through a surrogate mother. The elected surrogate had carried his baby and just put her to bed successfully.

That was the reason Tola had proceeded on maternity leave to care for her newborn child. I sat there numb as she enthused about how much the baby looks like her husband, how joyful he and her mother in-law were, I could only wonder at the selflessness of what she had arranged and achieved. I wondered without voicing it if this was her way of showing gratitude to her husband for sticking by her all those years. Whatever her reasons, I still think she did not have to do it, she was brave and selfless to have done it and she makes me so proud! The twinkle in her eyes that evening seemed to say "mission accomplished!" She looked so happy and fulfilled. I would say that is making lemonade when life serves you lemons!

Setbacks Do Have Their Uses

Setbacks are bound to happen at some point of each life. While most are private and may not have far-reaching effects and can easily be shrugged off, some botches are very public and can have life-changing impacts. The most important thing to bear in mind is that setbacks in themselves do not totally dictate the outcomes; it is the reaction of the subject, the lessons learnt and their application that set the direction and ultimate outcomes over time. While catastrophe can lead to immense hopelessness and depression, you must remain attentive to the lessons meant to be learnt therefrom. It is also useful to think through the events and actions that have led to a disaster, but that should not be excuse for undue doses of regret and self-pity. The point of the exercise is to separate what was a result of your own participation, errors and mistakes from those you had absolutely no control over. The acknowledgement of your contribution and errors provides an opportunity to improve life skills and for self-mastery. On the other hand, a deeper analysis of other contributors outside your control would help you to read external factors more accurately in future to better manage them.

'Life can only be understood backwards, but it must be lived forwards.'

—Kierkegaard

Experience and observation have shown me that when negative and pivotal things happen in a life, one of the most important and useful virtues needed for one not to be rendered hopeless is patience. The patience to allow circumstances unfold so that the events can be better understood backwards while nevertheless paddling forward. By this I mean avoiding being hamstrung by the critical event and missing out on enjoying the present or learning the lessons from the circumstance for future use. The usual reaction of freezing beyond the momentary calming to catch one's breath can result in a terrible spell of indecision and inability to take actions necessary for forward living. All effort must be made not to freeze or become a recluse after a trauma.

If you are able to understand and accept that what seemingly is a disruption could serve as the needed redirection or repositioning of life, you would be able, as painful as it might seem at the time, to embrace the full meaning of the situation. It is important at such times to be careful not to miss the opportunities presented to improve, change, get stronger, consider alternatives, and move on. The courage and ability to stand in the face of a disappointment to chart the way forward might be said to depend on the personality and temperament of each individual, but surely the alternative is a lack of faith in the self's ability to survive, prevail, and pull back from a gloomy downhill journey, which no one of any temperament should self-inflict. The reality is that the way to a fulfilling life is paved with a few skirmishes and setbacks, but to succumb to their negative effects is to rob yourself of the joyful and fulfilling life ahead. Setbacks, disappointments, or failure ought to be used as tools to propel you to a better future. Is Donald Trump not reputed to have been bankrupted four times to date?

Obama in his 'More perfect union' campaign speech encouraged us to be committed to "embracing the burdens of our past without becoming the victims of our past". There is no doubt that the historic does inform the future and it can sometimes be hard to break free of undeniably difficult occurrences that seek to continue to burden. But therein lies the opportunity and freedom to soar, not to become a victim. In the end, upheavals can bestow us with strengthening of spirit and humility by exposing aspects of our own selves never before imagined or understood. You can only become stronger from flexing; while we would all wish to go through life efficiently dodging disruptions, they do occur but we can let them teach us priceless lessons and lead us to pleasant places.

Some Lessons of Setbacks

The Resolve to Be Brave—Do Not Let Failure Become Fear

'Nothing splendid has ever been achieved except by those who dared believe that something inside of them was superior to circumstance.'

—Bruce Barton

In each life there are situations that create the opportunity for fearfulness when a misfortune is experienced. Some fears stem from experiences that are carried along and allowed to affect the present while some are new emotions aroused by impending events whether real or imagined. The element of courage is necessary to overcome the obstacles fear represents. It is important above all to remain clear thinking, not allowing the imagined images to take hold within your mind. Know that many difficult moments can be overcome by being rational and courageous. It is your decision to dig deep for that resolve to be brave. Once you choose to act with courage, the fear attached to whatever the situation is can usually be neutralised. Fear seeks a foothold within you, and only your resolve to be courageous tells it to vacate.

In the face of upheavals, it is by taking the initiative to reach within and become courageous to take positive actions rather than fearful reactions that you overcome the storm.

Seek and Accept Help

Recognising the 'trauma' effect, managing its emotional fallout, and getting the necessary help is the best process by which you can look after yourself after a traumatic experience. Help can be physical, psychological, or spiritual. Finding and using the right support system at such moments is critical and most beneficial. The post trauma stress, even when the drama is long gone is often underestimated, but their effect can continue for a much longer time span than is obvious to even the closest people to you. However, you must find ways of helping yourself and using external help. I remember waking up with huge anxiety pangs accompanied by palpitations for some years after the experience that redirected my career. Despite trying so hard to reason myself out of anxiety, I apparently missed the adrenaline rush of the deadlines, the structured days of the office, and the social interaction with clients and colleagues. The recognition of this post-traumatic stress and its management was key to my survival and ability to recover. I had to reintroduce similar structures into my new work life to claim my sanity back. Having become conditioned to working towards budgets, goals, and the dreaded appraisal system, I realised I had to introduce similar tools in my new line of work to regain a sense of purpose and achievement as I transitioned from being an employee to a business owner.

The initial reaction when life throws us a curve is to incubate and struggle to tackle the situation on your own. The resolve to be brave does not require you to deny yourself help and support that will stand you in good stead or provide the leverage needed to rise above the gloom and oppression that pervades at such a time. Resources for help abound in the form of family and friends just waiting to offer a hand-hold to help you get your footing back. Read the appropriate books, take counsel, and spend time with uplifting company.

You Can Recover — and This Too Shall Pass if You Let It

We all stumble. The point is not what caused you to do so; it is how you manage yourself in recovery that defines your gravitas. When you stumble, it is of importance to react from a position of self-awareness and intention to make a success of the future. Maya Angelou celebrates the courage of the human spirit over the harshest of obstacles and an ode to the power that resides in us all to overcome the most difficult circumstances is her collection of poems aptly titled "Touch Me, Life, Not Softly". An excerpt from my favourite of these poems, "I rise", says:

Up from a past that's rooted in pain

I rise

I'm a black ocean, leaping and wide,

Welling and swelling I bear the tide

Leaving behind nights of terror and fear

I rise

Unto a daybreak that's wondrously clear

I rise.

The lady wordsmith knew a thing or two about weathering the storm and coming out stronger as a result. The pride of knowing you could and you did; the chance to stand up tall at the face of life is a sweet feeling, and no one should ever taste the bitterness of setbacks without giving themselves a chance to savour that sweet feeling.

Stumbling Blocks to Recovery

Caged by Emotions

Arising from the ashes when life has happened to you hard can be made more difficult by the different emotions that burden as a result – anger, pride, sentimentality, or just pure shock from the surprise of it all. Any impediment to recovery is connected to one of these emotions and the earlier such underlying emotion is identified and dealt with, the faster you can be on your way out of the tunnel. Endeavour not to be caged in by fear, anger, pride, or shock. Shock is the body's biological coping strategy and in itself is short-lived and would pass once a person absorbs the realness of a situation. Shock can leave its mark but should not be a permanent hiding place.

Not Letting Go of the Past

'When one door closes another door opens; but we so often look so long and so regretfully upon the closed door, that we do not see the ones which open for us.'

—Alexander Graham Bell

Sentimentality is the greatest culprit when a person insists on holding onto the past or an old form of life when a paradigm shift is what is required. In the face of major life upsets, you must give yourself permission to believe there could be other and better ways. There is no reward in staying attention on something that might be lost for ever, only pain and lost opportunity.

Self-Pity and a Victim Mentality

It can be difficult to resist or shake off the victim's cloak when life appears to be unfair and conspiring against you. The wail of 'why always me!' is easy to become the mantra but the secret is to maintain the big-picture perspective of your life to reduce the import of a single occurrence. The earlier you get rid of self-pity, the faster you can get back in control. If Joseph in the Holy Bible were to take on the victim stance when his brothers and his master's wayward wife tried to impede his destiny, he would never have been propelled to the governorship of the land of Egypt.

Pride

Pride can be at the root of despising small beginnings when life shoots one down. Most people are unable to make a new start or see the opportunities lurking further down the path of a seemingly small beginning especially if there had been some success in the past. However, small beginnings do not necessarily mean a slow route to success as such beginnings can take accelerated momentum if there is enough passion and unwavering commitment to a new venture. I started a small housewares business after my banking career, which I decided to discontinue two years later mainly because of lack of synergy with my real estate business; however, very useful lessons were learnt from the experience, and it was a profitable stopgap not to be sniffed at.

Flourishing in the Aftermath with Lessons Learnt

It is often said that the best revenge when life deals its blow is to rise, brush oneself up, learn lessons of the experience, and go on to flourish. Remember, the monk says, "There are no mistakes, only lessons to be learnt. There is a purpose for everything that has ever happened to you and everything that will happen to you. Every experience offers lessons".

The ultimate aim and use of being brave in the face of adversity and recovering therefrom is to give yourself the chance to learn the lessons and flourish again. Armed with the life lessons learnt and the strength of character that the whole experience bestows, you will flourish.

Chapter 10 – Personal Success and Fulfilment

'Success Without Fulfilment is the Ultimate Failure'

—Tony Robbins

Have You Articulated That Life of Your Dreams

What does a successful life really mean or look like to you? That is the most important question you need to ask and answer about success. Too many people struggle through life never asking themselves that straight question. They easily equate a successful life to having more money or raising a family, perhaps driving a flashy car or having a house in the best part of town, without rigorously considering exactly how they would personally prefer to live their lives. Most people are so busy observing everybody else's life and wishing they were like X, Y, or Z, depending on how successful those people appear to be, going by media reports or gossip. Do you know what exactly would make your life fantastic in every possible way by your own reckoning? You need to know, because a successful life does not happen by accident, and you cannot work towards a goal that has not been set. A satisfying life is not inherited or assured by obtaining a degree, a top job, getting married (or divorced), having children, or retiring early. A great life is never about a formula. Surely money, a penthouse apartment, political power, or a loving family are wonderful things, but none of them by itself guarantees a satisfying life.

What each of us would consider a successful life has to be one that provides us the lifestyle that is satisfying and that has been chosen by us on purpose. Your on purpose life would have a central or unifying theme which people around you are likely to know you by. We all know that person who, despite living a different kind of life from what we believe to be fantastic but appears to be totally happy on his own terms. I recall being at a funeral recently and the theme of the life that had just passed away was obviously that of little deeds of beauty and contentment ... many people, friends and family alike, gave testimony that confirmed his satisfaction with the life he had chosen. His life was undeniably great and was invested in making its own contribution, using its talents and abilities to make an intended difference, no matter how small.

In considering the critical question, what does a successful life mean to you?, you might want to give a thought to the path you wish to tread and what legacy you wish to leave behind. It's good to do great things, but it's just as purposeful to do good things not so great, things that would give you that warm and satisfying pride and make you smile as the joy of it surprises you. That is fulfilment and personal success.

Once we know what is great by our own reckoning, I strongly believe that we each have the capability to create the fulfilling life we seek. Fulfilment is not reserved for the lucky few, the rich or the powerful. It is the birth right of every human being, whether we exercise our greatness in designing tall buildings or by teaching our children to stand tall. Fulfilment comes to us in different ways and means very diverse things to different people. This is why it is important that you sincerely define that basket of things that would fulfil you rather than measure the success of your life relative to another's. Your own talents, abilities, and resilience levels are common only to you and are designed to support the life that is great for you. But you need to first acknowledge what would make you personally joyful before you can articulate and work on building the life that would make it happen.

Your Own Balanced Scorecard—Defining Your Trophy

'Be yourself. Everyone else is already taken.'

—Oscar Wilde

Seeking your own personal success should be like creating a balanced scorecard for a business. It should not be success of an aspect at the detriment of other competing areas like the career or parenting dichotomy. It should be a form of having it all with a harmony that portrays your priorities and preferences. You should never buy the lie of totally giving up your dreams for the success of a singular aspect. Also, be cautious that youthful excitement and the lure and shine of 'living life to the fullest' do not becloud your view of later stages of life. The realisation of need for a balance comes much too late for many people when the excitement of youthful social life and work begins to subside. An early understanding that ultimate success and fulfilment requires many different aspects is most useful to achieve a satisfying balance.

Personal success specific to a life is the balanced score-card for that life. It is important that you define your trophy (as different from any other's). I ask that question again: What does a *great* or successful life really mean to you? This is where you must be ultra-candid with yourself and get clear in your mind what your own trophy would look like and the contents of its makeup. In playing to win, you need to define what winning means to you personally so that winning would ensure the satisfaction and fulfilment of your core values and needs. A person that ranks family, peaceful existence, privacy, and individuality high, for example, would not be fulfilled if he or she achieves immense professional success at the expense of family cohesion or privacy.

Be careful that you do not end up with a trophy that does not satisfy and is not so attractive when it is finally in your hand. Try to define the quality and content of your trophy ahead.

Your Own Trophy of Pleasing Balance

I have always been fascinated by the concept of balance in the measure of overall success. This might have been born of the fact of my gender or the generation and culture in which I grew up. My father's high expectations of me and my sister in terms of academics were always balanced by the cultural and societal expectation that we also kept an eye on achieving a family life. I therefore was always aware that there might be a need for balance from an early stage of life. There are competing aspects of life for all of us, female or male in any cultural setting. The challenge is for each person to have a clear view of their possible relative weighting and to consciously negotiate one's own middle ground or balance that would ultimately be fulfilling for them. It could be work/life balance, it could be high career/parenting balance; it could be financial gain/philanthropy balance – there are a myriad of these calls in anyone's life. It is your responsibility to analyse these and decide how to 'have it all' – albeit in satisfying proportions.

Personally, parenting became a most significant aspect, but despite being passionate about parenting, at no time did I consider giving up work totally. Yes, I slowed down at a point, and went part-time at another and became self-employed at an appropriate stage, but I always knew that fulfilling work and a positive sense of achievement is paramount to my personal wellbeing. The fact that my children are now grown without my ever having needed to give up work is the balance necessary for my harmony. I am pleased with the result of my not-so-straightforward route and the mix of work and parenting which has allowed me not to drop out of the professional terrain I enjoy. I would have had some regrets if I had totally sacrificed work for raising my children or if I had not done what I considered my duties in parenting for what may have been a higher-flying career. I am satisfied with my balance.

It is important to remain conscious and be careful of possible trade-offs that might not be intended. A super successful career at the expense of family life might not seem to be the trade-off being made when you are 30 and giving no thought to the fact that your life is all about work and not much else. Or, you might not be fully aware of the lifestyle choices you might unconsciously be making when you decide to increase your family size?

Harmony or what is considered balanced is as different for each of us as our DNA is different. Consciousness is what is required to ensure you are clear about the choices that are being made on the path of life towards achieving your own balance. The skew of balance that will fulfil you in the sometimes conflicting facets of life depends on your defined trophy. Such definition and consciousness will make you more deliberate in handling the different aspects for the whole to achieve that pleasing balance. This may require you to step down some aspects for others at different junctions of life; the freedom to travel might need to be curbed for future family provision; participation in an activity of personal interest might be limited by conflicting interests like family time. However, the concept of balance need not rob your life of joy because of the conflicting interests and the sacrifices you make, rather, the desired outcomes for which you plan and sacrifice should be a source of motivation and satisfaction.

Choosing Your Priorities for Success

'Everything worthwhile is uphill; downhill habits do not achieve uphill desires.'

—John Maxwell

The general principle of choosing priorities is that we can have what we choose, but not everything we want because our appetite will always exceed our grasp. Thanks to technology, you now have all the tools you need to do many things but it's unlikely that you can do all of them at once or in equal measures. You must choose: as a youngster, you must choose between partying all week long, indulging in alcohol, and missing university classes or living a moderate life of responsible attention to working for a good degree. Health-wise, you must choose between a healthy lifestyle of exercises and a decent diet or that of a couch potato with an unhealthy diet of grease and refined foods. Financially, you have the choice between being disciplined to plan for a robust future and unthinkingly wasting away money on holidays and restaurant meals that you can hardly afford. In each of these situations the outcomes of your decisions are different, but the choices leading to each outcome must be made by you. And most of the repercussions will be borne by you.

Once your priorities and choices are unmistakable, life becomes orderly, and your time can be spent doing the things you have defined and chosen, investing yourself in what will make you a winner at the game of life. Joy and happiness come from deciding who we want to be, what we value, the outcomes we desire, and making choices that support and prioritize those things.

This is the point when many people get into trouble. They declare their values and define the great life they would love but are unable to support these with disciplined actions and prioritising. They can be said to have uphill hopes and desires but downhill habits. They value and desire ambition and a comfortable retirement, but by their action and priority, they appear to actually value fun-seeking, being a couch potato, the short-term satisfaction of expensive new cars and unaffordable holidays even more. The big challenge is how to make sure your daily actions and priority actually reflect your values and long term goals. Many people are able to articulate their five- or even ten-year goals, but their actions, their daily to-do list, and their short-term plans belies their long-term goals. Be careful to consciously ensure that you do not have such conflicts between your intentions and actions. Remember, hope is not a strategy. Having defined your desired great life and planned towards it, you are required to work and walk your plan. Nothing worthwhile has been achieved without having been intentionally desired and worked for.

Most ambitious people know they should formalise their plans and have written goals and strategies to attain them, but many ordinarily bright people snigger at its cheesiness. The fact is, it is easier for your daily actions to accurately reflect your priorities when you have a clear plan and strategy. You would not be likely to procrastinate, and it would be easier to make the right choices that will help you win big at your game. You would not be chasing your uphill desires with down-hill habits.

You Need Propelling Purpose for Success

'This is the true joy in life, the being used for a purpose recognized by yourself as a mighty one.... What I do makes me joyful because I consider my outcomes a measure of success.'

—George Bernard Shaw

Finding a purpose or purposes beyond achieving the usual measures of success such as fame, wealth, and desired lifestyle ranks high in ultimately adjudging oneself personally successful, an impactful purpose beyond the self. Purposeful people tend to say by their lives "There is a reason and good need for why I am here and do what I do; I am not going around aimlessly". Your personal purpose is what you spend your life doing that makes your stay on earth fruitful and relevant. It is that mission that you are meant to accomplish, the contribution that makes your life and existence profitable to the universe. Purpose makes you transcend the idea of just being alive, or just toiling for a living; it is about finding something to live passionately for. Life is not an accident, it is a sum total of purposeful or purposeless actions we have taken and will take. When a life has no purpose, the person is likely to go on an aimless pursuit of things that seem good to have. A purposeful life, on the other hand, will define you, your relationships, and your pursuits.

Your Purpose Is Found As You Keep Evolving

When people talk about finding their purpose in life, one gets the impression that they expect there to be only one purpose, well defined from the get-go and for all times, for life. This in itself can make it difficult to live with assuredness and enthusiasm as the constant and elusive search for purpose becomes central to a life. My observation however is that we and our purpose(s) tend to evolve from time to time.

I was intrigued recently when my friend Bala, who, at middle age, has had an uncommonly successful and eventful life, asked me what I think he should do with his life. Of course he was asking not about his whole life but the remaining segment he was about to commence after just successfully completing a national assignment in which he was outstandingly successful. As we discussed and worked through possibilities, we took into consideration his experiences, personal desires, and temperament while acknowledging situations and developments out of his control. That discussion and the process of trying to find him a fresh purpose underscored what I had always wondered at and suspected: that our purpose(s) can only be fully achieved if we are willing to keep evolving and reinventing ourselves as necessary over a lifetime.

I know I have continued to evolve, having spent the first fifteen years post-graduation in accounting and consulting practice, followed by an eight-year stint in a banking career, and then transformed to doing a mixed bag of commercial activities including real estate investments, consulting, and teaching. I see how all those different experiences serve me today and find purpose for me on company boards, in life coaching and mentoring, and now in philanthropy.

The purpose(s) of each life do not reside only in one facet or segment of it. It appears that my friend and I, while moving from one season to another, are yet to fully identify and fulfil all of our purpose; more purpose could be waiting to evolve as life progresses. Your purpose(s) are found at different stages of life and become recognizable to you as you are able to evolve over time, bringing along experiences to enrich later activities. The experiences of your particular journey and your willingness to keep evolving will lead you to those purposes.

A Purposeful Life Makes a Difference— Just like the Starfish Thrower!

The story of the starfish thrower underscores how small differences matter. The starfish thrower was walking on a beach after a storm, throwing starfish back into the ocean so they wouldn't die on the shore from the heat of the sun. Someone present at the scene wondered why he wasted his time, noting there were millions of starfish, that he couldn't possibly throw them all back, and the few he saved wouldn't make any real difference. The starfish thrower silently bent over, picked up, and threw another starfish into the surf and replied, "It made a difference for that one starfish!"

Whether we express our uniqueness in business or music, in parenting, or in any of the thousands of "small" ways that are often overlooked, but which are absolutely essential, purposefulness makes a difference. Most people remember a special teacher, or a grandmother who taught them to read. Perhaps there was a neighbour who encouraged you when things were hard going. All these people would have made some significant impacts, such impacts are the purposes of their participation. We all therefore have the opportunity and the challenge, to make a difference and to live a life that changes the world for those we touch.

There is much fulfilment in making a difference and touching lives, and it doesn't matter how few you help; it makes a difference to them.

Purpose never mistakes activity for impact. A life of purpose announces itself by the difference it makes, and it is the conviction and impact of purpose that is the starting point of personal success.

The Traits That Power Success

What are the characteristics that increase your chances at achieving long-term success? I have observed that some traits recur in the lives of unusually successful people. The wonderful news is that those traits are learnable and can be developed by anyone who considers them desirable and is willing to make some effort. The following traits will serve well on the road of success:

Being a Magnet for Success

Sure, being in the right place at the right time, knowing the right people, and being born to privilege can all be success factors, but the overriding truth is that ultimately, the course of our lives has more to do with who we are as people than with what opportunities come our way. Being a magnet for good things stems from who you are in yourself and how you portray yourself to the rest of the world. In the first place, the way you view the chances that come your way and how you handle them depends on your personality and thoughts. The reason some people have a long line of failures is because they lack the character, that would produce the kind of fruit they seek. What keeps them from realizing the success they desire is their character, their person, and how others perceive them, not necessarily as they imagine themselves to be. To avoid self-sabotage (albeit unintentional) with the opportunities that life presents, be it the best jobs, fulfilling relationships, or other desirable things, it is your responsibility to prepare yourself to be already able to deliver on the kind of things you wish to be entrusted with. You have to become that person or candidate that would attract the attention of an employer you would prefer to work for. The sooner you stop hoping for some kind of miracle and begin to work on the personhood that will produce the results and attract the kind of attention you desire in your life, the closer you will be to success.

The key to becoming a magnet for success is continuous personal development and refinement to make you ready for the next opportunity on your path. Some of the preparation or improvement of self may seem like hardships, but in grappling with these, you grow character and keep reinventing yourself for success. You might have noticed a phenomenon such that as soon as you gained a new skill and understanding, it seems just then opportunities arise that need exactly those skills and in taking those opportunities, you are propelled to a higher level of achievement. You will find that you are able to attract to your life what you are prepared and ready for. As you work to make yourself a magnet, your life direction will begin to feed from your improving self, attracting success to you.

Personal Stability and Orderliness

High achievers usually live quiet, structured, almost boring lives. They tend to settle down, have good relationships, and mind their own business. They do not fall victim to addictions, fads, or impulses. There is purpose and structure to their lives. They keep good hours, eat well, get some exercise, and have an organised financial status. They do not allow the background of their life to interfere with achieving their goals. Boring is good for this purpose! Undue and constant excitement in life is distracting and takes away attention from what is important. In the end, an orderly life leading to success is easier to achieve than a complicated and disorganised life. The latter can be tasking making a person unwell and unattractive to others for collaboration.

Self-Direction and Responsibility

Many successful people possess a sense of the direction in which they are headed; whether it's regarding small things or a long-term vision, they know what they want and permit few distractions. They are not tempted by shortcuts; once they have decided on their direction or purpose, they point straight ahead and hold themselves responsible for their actions and outcomes. Successful people also tend to take responsibility for their situation, whether good or bad, and acknowledge it to be the result of their own past thoughts, actions, or mistakes.

Personal Urgency

Urgency should never be confused with impatience or all motion without progress. Successful people will in fact be found to be patient, persistent, and cautious, but they do not waste time. They think in terms of priorities and action plans that propel forward, not activity for the sake of activity.

Constant Learning

High achievers are curious and tend to read more, ask questions of those who should know, and scrutinise things. They of course make mistakes, but rarely the same mistake twice and not too often. You will find that people who are successful at something actually make the effort to learn to do them right, be it investing or sports. They also seek mentors or advisors, because they understand that practical experience and knowledge can be invaluable and they don't have to reinvent the wheel.

Most of us were not born with organised lives, a sense of self-direction, or urgency. These are habits that you can learn and master if you so desire and pay attention. Success is about exhibiting conducive traits, learning appropriate skills, and applying them to the job at hand.

Weaknesses That Can Hold You Back

Just as certain character traits propel to success, there also are those that can limit or hold a person back from his or her potential. Some of these are considered below.

Lack of clarity and focus. Many people sort of muddle through life. They have some hopes or wishes, perhaps some images or expectations in their mind, but they never truly define their outcomes in advance. If you are currently in this group, take time to make clear exactly what you want. Write them down, and tell your confidants for personal accountability so they can tell you to get on with them when you get distracted. There are other people who are clear about what they want, but are too lazy or undisciplined, and maybe fearful such that they never seriously lay claim to their trophies. They want to achieve a goal, but they also want too many other things that distract them from focussing their time and effort. They engage in too many things that are not in sync with their goal. An intending marathon runner who undermines his body with junk food and tiring social engagements is surely not billed for success.

Mistaking hope for strategy. If you would like a raise in pay, you have to find out from the boss exactly what is required to get it. Too many people hope for an outcome but never devise a strategy to make it happen. You are not going to arrive at your target weight if you have not worked out the diet and exercise regime to get you there. When you set a goal, you make a plan and then work out how to achieve it. That's having a strategy, not just hoping. Two very different things.

'Fear of failure. You've got to jump off cliffs and build your wings on the way down.'

—Annie Dillard.

Granted, a reckless dabbling at things you do not understand would be a waste of time; but baseless fear should not be allowed to hold you back from embarking on the expedition to your dreams. Once you have done your research, learnt all you can, sought counsel as needed, and obtained the inputs required, then you must jump off that cliff. Many things would not have been invented or created left to the fear of failure.

Procrastination. How 'soon, not now' becomes 'never'. William Shakespeare in *Julius Caesar* says, "There is a tide in the affairs of men which taken at the flood, leads on to fortune. Omitted, all the voyage of their life is bound in shallows and in miseries. On such a full sea are we now. And we must take the current when it serves, or lose our ventures."

In achieving success in whatever path we choose, time and chance can bring great opportunities and challenges. Awareness and sensitivity of the happenings around you coupled with the knowledge of what you really want out of life should mean you do not miss your opportunities. Procrastination is the bane of most opportunities. Procrastination is nothing but the postponement of necessary action. It is simply avoiding something we don't want to do. The benefits an action could be apparent to you but if a sense laziness or discomfort about doing it holds you back, you will procrastinate.

The dire consequences of procrastination is best depicted by Stephen Mansfield in his book *The Faith of Barack Obama*, in discussing Obama's bid for the presidency of the United States in 2008. He underscored how life offers opportunities that must be recognised and then embraced in a timely fashion. In his words, "To do so leads to glory; to fail to recognise the destined moment is to remain in the shallows; in the immobility of low tide; in the miserable contemplation of what might have been".

There is no shortage of desire and hope, the problem is in backing them up with the required action. If you have thought it up and desired it, get going with the required actions if you are to achieve your desire. Time and chance happen to us all – seize yours!

Some Themes of Achieving Personal Success

The March to Greatness Is Rarely a Dash

We often hear about overnight success stories of sudden fame and extraordinary breakthroughs. They make us wonder what we can do to bring us our own fame and extraordinary success. Most of those 'overnight' successes, however, did not happen overnight; the news of the success just happened to break overnight. There would have been some very hard work, the 10,000 hours, usually in obscurity, over a fairly long time with some failures along the way until their moment in the sun arrives. The reality and backstories seldom match the impression we get from the breaking news.

Jim Collins's book *Great by Choice* is a study of the discipline of companies who significantly outperform their competition. In the book he recounts the experience of Roald Amundsen and Robert Scott, two men who raced each other to the South Pole in 1911.

Amundsen was slow, methodical, and disciplined, limiting himself to travelling only twenty miles a day, even when the weather was perfect and he could have gone further. Daily, he covered his planned twenty miles and made camp. Even in very good weather he kept to the discipline of twenty miles, allowing him and his team to rest and repair their equipment. When the weather was terrible, they were strong enough to cope with the conditions and still achieved their twenty miles a day.

Scott, on the other hand, was the typical competitive adventurer. He moved as quickly as he possibly could, using the opportunity of good weather to push faster and further to the goal. When exhaustion or bad weather slowed him down, he only pushed himself and his team extra hard to make it up when the weather permitted.

Eventually, the race ended differently for the two men. The methodical and disciplined Amundsen won the race to the pole by more than thirty days. Scott arrived at the peak to find a letter left for him by Amundsen. Unfortunately, the real lesson from the story was that Scott and his party froze to death on the return journey just a few miles short of their supply camp and safety. This is the real-life version of that old children's tale of the tortoise and the hare.

Collins was making the point that greatness is usually the result of patient planning, discipline, and commitment that successful companies like Intel and other winning companies adopt to consistently outperform their competition. They avoid the flash in the pan in favour of consistent results through discipline. This does not mean that sudden big bangs do not occur once in a while, but they cannot be the basis of seeking long-term success. Indeed, the march to success is rarely a dash.

Social Mobility—Reinventing Self

'I'm so proud of my humble background that the subtitle of my autobiography will be Thank Heavens I Was Born Poor.'

—Countess Marta Marzotto of Italy

Any discussion about success would not be complete without the consideration of the social strings that hold back anyone whose incidence of birth was humble. The healthiest psyche that a person from humble beginnings should have is that portrayed by Countess Marta. That first battle of the mind must be won, and the same mental strength that makes that possible will propel a person to achieve upward social mobility if they so desire. When a person has grown up with humble means where envisioning, an enabling environment, and opportunities for success are in short supply, the effort and mind-set needed to propel themselves out of poverty and to aspire to a good measure of success can be enormous. For such, the examples of success are observed from so far that it is almost impossible to seem easy to emulate and the mind pictures that should feed vision are mostly sketched by the immediate surroundings, making it difficult to boldly aspire.

However, "Your background must not determine your future!" were the words of encouragement Michelle Obama spoke to some girls from an inner London school visiting Oxford University with her in a bid to envision them. She told them that they too belong in Oxford, after all, she herself, a good example and product of social mobility, found her way to Princeton and Harvard.

Upward social mobility is a reward for reinventing efforts and the only limit to reinvention is the self because the aspiration and effort required are self-propelled. While a helping hand is always useful for self-improvement, social mobility is easier than most people imagine. All that is required is for a pilgrim to decide to leave his or her current location and take the steps to head for a desired higher and better destination. It is that desire, decision and effort that are pivotal to social mobility. But it does happen. You just need to make a personal decision to leave your current place for a better place, and you immediately begin to 'see' a vision of the Promised Land. Once you have that vision, the rest, if not easy, is possible!

Managing Success

Adapting a song with similar wordings, the question is: Now that you've found success, what are you going to do with it? There are various consequences of wealth and success beyond one's own sense of accomplishment and some of these need understanding and conscious management if they were not to make what should be an enjoyable state tedious or even damaging. When you have found success, I know a few things you should be prepared to confront, tame, or manage. Greed and pride are examples of those to be tamed while your relationships would require some management. The following are some pitfalls to bear in mind.

Contentment Is Great Gain

It is usually said that success is a journey, not a destination. You will find this to be so as you achieve the goals you have set and maybe exceed them. Be careful though, as you continue that journey, to know contentment. Greed is its own punishment. It is the unquenchable craving for an ever-shifting goal of world measures that are not fulfilling in themselves. A lot of people grieve at the pain of reaching each mountaintop just to find it empty of joy and fulfilment. True success is liberating when you find detachment from success labels and free yourself to an abundant life that is not defined by things. Contentment is truly great gain for your peace of mind.

Another gain of contentment is its help in avoiding the trap of the mirage of perfection that is never achieved. There is a wonderful quote about Howard Hughes, that for all his genius, wealth, and determination, "He sought a perfection that assured failure". One must not do that to oneself. A better balance is to strive for excellence achievable by one's talents and abilities, a satisfying personal success, not perfection.

Don't Take Yourself Too Seriously

Keeping grounded and not taking yourself too seriously can become a great challenge once success arrives. If you were to live by the size of your bank balance or your celebrity status, you are likely to become a different person barely recognisable to yourself and your old friends. It is important that you have a system of reality check in the form of close friends and family if you are not to be overtaken by the grandeur syndrome from a bloated ego. You should remain accountable to at least one person who is able to call your attention to unsavoury changes in your personality and help you manage it.

Relationships Can Become Tricky!

One of the most difficult fallouts of success is the change it can bring to your relationships, especially with family and friends. It is common to see even spousal dynamics change as one party becomes very successful. The successful partner needs to be more sensitive about the insecurity the other half might be experiencing. With friends and family, arrogance is too quickly ascribed to actions that might have been overlooked in the past. With success comes the responsibility to be more cautious and sensitive in relating to and discerning the feelings of other people.

The Pursuit of Happiness

'Happiness is that state of consciousness which proceeds from the achievement of one's values.'

—Anonymous

There is a strong connection between happiness and success. Happiness is one of the indications of a successful life and, going by the above quote, it follows that success by your own reckoning should be a major contributor to your happiness. A good indication of how happy you are is what you think or say to yourself last thing at night and first thing in the morning. Successful people tend to be thankful because they have had satisfying outcomes and greet a new day with enthusiasm. Achievement of self-set goals is common to both success and happiness.

'Happiness does not depend on outward things but on the way we see them.'

—Leo Tolstoy

Beyond task completion and achievement, the truth is you feel the way you think. That is why beautiful, accomplished, and successful people can lack contentment and self-esteem and remain in a deeply unfulfilled state. Their thinking is consumed with negative views about themselves and their lives. People can also be robbed of joy by negative emotions like anger and envy. As they compare themselves to others who appear to be more confident and successful, they condemn themselves for not matching up to the Joneses, little knowing what the Joneses are grappling with and feeling.

Dramas can build up a constant atmosphere of negativity because one is focused upon outside disruptions. Nevertheless, according to Tolstoy, it is up to you to decide the views you take of them. That's right, your thoughts and not the actual events create your moods. Though it can seem like happiness is down to circumstances, how you think about them and how you react play the more important role.

Choice to Be Happy

'There is only one way to happiness, and that is to cease worrying about things which are beyond the power of our will.'

—Epictetus

As happiness is a state of your mind, you have the freedom to choose happiness; intentionally choosing happiness is being mindful of a sincere desire to be happy; it is to knowingly avoid negative thoughts that if repeated can sink into the subconscious mind and become habitual. Both unhappiness and happiness are habits. It is possible to be depressed, dejected, and unhappy for long enough and become accustomed to the mental patterns of unhappiness to form a habit of it. Very few of us will get through life without experiencing some episodes of anxiety, anger, worry, or depression. We will encounter some frustrations and losses, and we will make mistakes. However, we can all learn to handle difficult situations and emotions through training our minds in compassion. Maintaining a compassionate stance towards ourselves and other people can help us gain better perspective, be less judgmental, and enhance our own well-being.

Happiness is the harvest of a quiet, companionate, and grateful mind, and you have the freedom to desire happiness. Just as you might work on your health or fitness, you can give yourself a happiness regime and environment. If you take note of what makes you feel good over time and then make an effort to schedule in more of these things, you'd experience happiness more frequently. Try to include exercise in that regime; it's a proven mood booster. Quality relationships also protect against depression, so make relating to loving family and good friends a priority. Appreciate what you have and find reason to be grateful by making a list of the good things that happen to you and these needn't be earth-shattering, they could be as simple as enjoying a cup of tea with a friend or by yourself in peaceful solitude.

There have been moments when I needed to drag my thoughts and demeanour away from deeply depressing matters to one of gratitude and joy, and this is not to say I get into denial of whatever challenges and situations there might be. I simply make a choice in spite of that to remain positive, thereby giving myself a chance to return to the happy state. You can be happy by choice when you consciously and intentionally keep joyful. Only one person in the world can make you feel unhappy, worried, or depressed and that person is *you*. You are mostly in control of your happiness.

Propel Your Future Success with the Past!

We can fuel our future dreams and empower the future by 'borrowing' confidence from our past achievements and successes. Therefore, celebrate your achievements and use them as a compass, knowing, deep inside, that you have the ability to boldly go wherever you wish in the future. And then proceed to live an even more successful life!

Chapter 11 – Sound Body and Mind

'A sound mind in a sound body is a short but full description of a happy state in this world.'

—John Locke

Consider for a moment how successful your life can feel if you are unhealthy in body or mind. Would you have full enjoyment of your achievements or worldly riches if body, mind, or both are troubled? Conversely, how do you find the power to actively and intentionally live if you are constantly lethargic, ill, or of an unsound mind? Whatever else you are doing and striving at, it is advisable that you don't forget the backdrop of it all, your health.

It is often said that a healthy body is a godly one. The root of this saying is in religiosity, an attempt perhaps to encourage the brethren to shun the excesses of the flesh such as gluttony, alcoholism, laziness, and all, such. Nevertheless, encouraging a healthy lifestyle is good no matter the source of the advice.

The 'health is wealth' slogan also underscores the importance of health in the scheme of things. Good health is a most invaluable asset without which all else is nought. If it is however that obvious that a sound body and mind are prerequisite for the enjoyment of life and all life has to offer, it is strange that the discipline to avoid excesses and engage in health promoting activities does not come easily to many of us. The animal kingdom, by default, eats what is good for them; they do not abuse alcohol and other substances and would probably exercise for pleasure! If humans only took some example from the animals, all would be well, and there would be no need for the growing industry in health management and research on the causes of many diseases and how to avoid them.

A Healthy Body—It's All about Habit

Exercise

I had always tried to exercise, albeit fitfully. From about my mid teens I began to pile on some weight, but it was never a big problem as I would usually lose some by going on some diet and starting a new regime of exercise. So I was no stranger to necessary exercise – necessary for weight loss. Work and family commitments of course had priority, and regular exercise was the first activity to be dropped if I became too busy. I exercised only the way you would take prescription medication when absolutely necessary if you became ill.

That went on until aged 48. I signed up for a boot camp to lose weight to fit into a dress for a party. The particular seven-day boot camp, apart from rigorous exercises and starvation diet, included talks meant to address bad health habits learnt over a lifetime. On day five of boot camp, we all watched the trainer we had aptly named Sergeant Pain walk into the lecture room during a thirty-minute break from hard labour. What could he possibly say that he had not barked out on the training ground? He sat at the desk like a professor and said he had a few questions for us and would appreciate raising of hands so he could identify who spoke ... typical!

The first question was, "Do you regularly wake up in the morning and ask of yourself if you should or would eat that day?' Ha, trick question! That was about food and nutrition, not exercise, and he was not the nutrition instructor. Probably more from tiredness than rudeness, we all stared at him with no hands shooting up. Then he asked how many people planned vigorous exercise three days a week, and a few hands shot up. Then he wanted to know the four-days-a-week people, and I joined this group (I did plan to exercise four times a week even if it did not always work according to plan). He even had some hands raised for five days a week. He then said something very profound, at least to me, which has changed my attitude to exercise forever, though it was not inventive wisdom. The summation of his lecture was: The body was made to move and work but it is necessary that we eat in order to fuel and nourish it for those activities. He asked why humans eat despite having no plan to physically move or exercise to use up the fuel they load up on. He explained how not aligning food intake to our physical activities is the only reason we put on weight. He wondered why humans naturally plan meals as daily enjoyable activity but make no daily plan for some exercise commensurate with their food intake. He likened lack of regular exercise of a body to a machine or car made for moving that would lose conditioning in its moving parts if left dormant. A body is burdened by the lack of exercise, and that burden is greater when it is also fed beyond its needs. He wondered why many people do not consider exercise beneficial and enjoyable.

That talk changed my motive for exercise from vanity or the need to shed some weight to that of a necessary and beneficial regular activity that should be planned for and enjoyed. In your mission to get fit, start by choosing an activity that you like, and find a team, if possible. Team sports is an effective way of exercising and is great for making new friends to keep you motivated and for accountability. By going with a friend to fitness class, gym, or boot camp, you get moral support and can socialize while becoming healthier and fitter.

Time commitment for regular exercise, especially while raising a young family or working all hours in a career, can be the easy excuse for giving up; but you can consciously build in veritable exercise into everyday activities. You need not wait until you are clad in lycra and hit the gym; simple choices can be just as effective. Take the stairs and walk everywhere! Make the most of your day by walking to lunch or skipping emailing work colleagues in favour of short walks to discuss work matters with them. Light, post-meal exercise, like walking, can lower your blood sugar and prevent your body from storing fat. As long as you keep moving after you eat, you will reap similar benefits, doing the dishes or completing other household tasks count. It is not so difficult to help yourself get strong, fit, and energized. Every day, make a habit of some fitness activity even if for only fifteen minutes, and over time that minimum investment will pay good dividends. But only if you persist and it becomes a habit.

Healthy Eating Can Be Enjoyable Too!

I have become a big fan of eating from a place of empowerment and self-control rather than from the corner of being denied. It is important that Healthy eating is not only enjoyable, but also does not have to be complicated with measuring spoons and calorie counting; in fact, the simpler the model, the likelier your keeping to it and your success. Keep it simple and focus on understanding what healthy food choices look like and how they help to promote your wellbeing. If, for example, when you have a true craving and must have something sweet, it is not a case of, "I can't have the chocolate cake"; rather, it's "I can have the blueberries with a small amount of the chocolate cake", and then you do not feel denied. That would allow you realize your power to choose, and it becomes much easier to have a smaller slice of cake.

Your objective should be to become mindful of eating to fuel your body rather than gorging on whatever is available. That mind-set eventually becomes second nature so that you are not thinking about food all the time or feel deprived. You then begin to intuitively eat foods that nourish you and make you feel much better. Certainly, some foods make you feel better while some drain you; if you listen to your body, you would realize sugar- and animal fat-laden meals leave you lethargic long before they lay down the belly fat. The vegetables, salads, proteins and good oils, on the other hand, are satisfying and keep your digestive system healthy while protecting your body from many diseases.

Sugar, fat, and refined foods are the enemy and it should be noted that most convenient and fast foods are full of them. During one of my weekly food shopping trips, a young lady who was quite overweight shyly asked me if I actually enjoy the foods I was about to pay for. She genuinely appeared not to imagine how broccoli, cauliflower, peppers, and lean proteins could be enjoyable. In the half minute I had without slowing down the queue and irritating the checkout staff, I tried to let my young friend see how nourishing those are and how good preparation and spicing can make all the difference when it comes to taste. No mention was made about her weight during the exchange, we concentrated on the possibility of making a habit of healthy eating!

Your Body Weight—Taking Control

The reason words like battle and fighting come up when discussing the tackling of excess weight is because you do those things until you gain control of managing your body weight. Getting to a healthy body weight can feel like a battle, but the good news is that it can be achieved and maintained if you desire it and take control in your mind. If you're overweight, it is most likely you got there by bad eating habits. Changing to healthy habits is what is required to take you where you want to be. Again, it's about goals, planning, and working the plan. It is about remaining conscious of your actions to become the weight that is healthy and at which you feel confident.

There is no shortage of new fads, pills, and more for losing weight. All promise to be revolutionary and create a new you. Some work and some don't. Scientific findings also change and confuse; some years ago, trans fat, a dangerous manmade lipid found in margarine, was thought to be healthier than regular fats. But by the mid-1990s, public health journals revealed the opposite to be true. If even the scientists sometimes get it wrong, it is safe to say that understanding the nuances of nutrition can be tricky and hard to follow. The least confusing route to achieving a healthy body weight is to ignore trends and fads, and instead focus on healthy eating strategies and habits and to stick to them. No matter what occasional blunders you might make, you will then be more likely to keep yourself on the trim and healthy road. You can avoid a lifetime of losing and regaining weight by learning how to eat, not how to diet. Losing weight isn't easy, but neither is it difficult. It takes commitment, discipline, and for many, a complete lifestyle makeover. Making healthier food choices coupled with regular exercise will kick start your weight loss and if stayed with for long enough would become a lifelong habit.

Here are some healthy habits I have found useful in my many weight loss battles, which if built into your daily routine should result in shedding excess weight.

- *Eating a light and early dinner.* This does magic in the weight struggle. If you stop eating three hours before you hit the sack, and make that last meal a light and healthy one, your body is better primed to burn fat instead of creating more while you sleep. It is simple science: your body does not need fuel to sleep and would only use late dinners to lay down fat.

- *Make a habit of weighing yourself regularly.* That must be why it is called 'watching your weight'! I know more than anyone else that stepping on the scale can sometimes be disheartening, particularly after a weekend of treats, but it's best to bravely face the music and reset. Monitoring your weight keeps your mind on your health and prevents denial that can mean going too far out in the wrong direction before you know it. If you are the sort that the numbers on the scale make you drown your sorrow in more comfort eating, you might not do a daily ritual but you must allow yourself at least a weekly weigh-in. Be mindful as you weigh that you could be building fat-burning muscles that can keep the numbers up a bit if you have just taken up muscle building exercise.

- *Plan your meals ahead and keep healthy food on hand.* Build a routine for mealtimes. If you find yourself scratching your head every day when the clock strikes noon, wondering what to have for lunch, you are likely to end up eating impulsively and taking in more calories than if you planned ahead for a healthy meal. Thinking ahead the healthy option to have when eating out or with friends is a good strategy if you dine out often. Also, have handy healthy snacks like nuts and pre-cut vegetables in your fridge to help you make the healthiest choice when you need to snack.

- *Reward yourself.* Once you've established a healthy routine, you need to establish a reward system or a cheat day; think of a land of milk and honey after a journey of tedium. A great way to stick to a healthy diet without breaking down into a rebellious binge-mode is to reward yourself with a small favourite food once or twice a week. Pick a food you love and treat yourself to a small portion of about two hundred calories. But remember, you only get the reward if you deserve it, and the keyword is *small*.

- *Please eat breakfast!* Regularly skipping breakfast makes you more likely to be obese. They don't call it the most important meal of the day for nothing. Eating a nutritious breakfast of a healthy balance of protein and fibre, like eggs with fruit and whole wheat toast jumpstarts your metabolism and prevents you from overindulging throughout the day. Some thinking argues it is okay to skip breakfast to mimic fasting in order to lose weight, but it's not. Your bodyweight benefits from fasting for about twelve hours overnight, but better to let the fasting be mostly before bedtime and sleep time rather than in the morning when you need your metabolism to support your daily activities.

- *Drink water, and lots of it!* Sixty per cent of your body is water, which makes it vital to every important metabolic process. Quenching thirst with sugar-laden beverages is one of the easiest ways to gain belly fat. Replace some of your soda, beer, or juices intake with water, and you would soon see the benefits.

- *Intermittent fasting.* There is scientific evidence of good weight management and promotion of improved gut health resulting from intermittent fasting. The most popular routine is the 16 hour fasting on a daily basis but there are other fasting routines like fasting for one day a week that are equally beneficial to health. One of the great outcomes of fasting is weaning oneself off mindless snacking.

- *Manage stress.* Stress is not exercise. It wears your mind out rather than your body. Work-, relationship-, or family-related stress can lead to weight gain simply because a stressed body releases cortisol, a hormone that promotes abdominal fat storage. Coupled with that is you could be taking solace in food when stressed – and not just any food but comforting ones that are usually sweet or fried.

- *Eat more protein.* Protein increases lean muscle mass, which keeps your metabolism running on high, even when you're resting. Protein also keeps you full, making you most unlikely to overeat. Aim to include protein like fish, eggs, lean meats, beans, low-fat dairy products, and nuts in all your meals and snacks.

- *Keep the big picture in mind.* Life happens. The unexpected often occurs no matter how much preparation we make to avoid it. When you occasionally make poor decisions and slip up on your eating plan, you must consciously reset and get back on track. We are not perfect, nor will we ever be. Temporary lapses should not lead to ruining all your progress because healthy eating doesn't ruin itself in instantaneous moments. Keep the big picture in mind, knowing that your healthy lifestyle is for the long term.

Some Health Matters to Be Mindful Of

Smoking is insanely bad for you. No one who has suffered the addiction ever wishes they could have smoked more. Those who get heart disease, cancer, and lung disorder from smoking wish they had listened to those badgering relatives and doctors. If you don't smoke now, don't even think about starting! If you do, quitting is the project for saving your life. All kinds of techniques are now available to support quitting and a smoker should consider one of them.

Alcohol Abuse: Enjoying a couple of glasses of wine, beer, or some cocktail is not in itself a dangerous pastime. However, when you regularly drink beyond the medically suggested maximum units or past the point of conscious enjoyment and into a stupor, you ought to seek help for alcoholism. Beyond intoxication and the general accompanying embarrassing behaviour, the real problem with excessive drinking is that alcohol abuse use ultimately damages the liver. Of course, there are examples of people drinking heavily into their eighties, and this may be due to a lucky predisposition, and no one can tell ahead if they are predisposed to liver cancer until it happens!

Oral Hygiene: Beyond the bright and pearly smile, regular brushing, flossing, and visit to the dentist can actually save your life. People with gum disease have been found to have a higher risk of heart problems, stroke, diabetes, pneumonia, and some cancers. The dentist and hygienist would clean your teeth and gums, remove any build-up of scale and show you the effective way to brush and floss. The cynical amongst us, myself included for many years, should not consider the expense of dental care a waste just because our teeth don't show any obvious signs of trouble yet.

Leisure and Recreation: We spend most of life in activities of daily living – work, sleep, social duties – but we ought to make some time for leisure time free from life commitments. Allowing yourself to play and relax can often be a distant thought and any intentions somehow slip through your fingers because of the frenetic pull to work and other obligations. While a common perception is that leisure is just spare time not consumed by the necessities of living, it has been found to allow us take time apart to reflect on the values and realities of daily life, and therefore an essential element of personal development. The downtime to recharge the batteries in fact makes for improved work performance. The ability to afford the time and resources for leisure is one of the purposes of work, making leisure a reward in itself. Leisure contributes immensely to our physical and psychological well-being.

Grooming: We each have a level of innate or learnt vanity that affects how much grooming we believe we require and make an effort to get. My grandmother made grooming such an important 'chore' when I was growing up by drilling it into our heads that "You are met as you arrive". That is a translation of a Yoruba statement that is similar but not exactly same as the English "First impressions count". In the Yoruba context, it conjures the importance of not misrepresenting oneself and therefore being shabbily treated by others because of a bad appearance. It underscores your ability, through grooming, to affect how the day would go and the respect that you would command and enjoy because of your appearance. A well-groomed person enjoys an enthusiasm to engage from society. Well-cut or styled hair, well-manicured nails, pleasant fragrance, smart dressing, clean teeth, and fresh breadth all contribute to a well-groomed presentation.

Mental Health—Minding the Mind

Worry and Mindfulness

Often in moments of chaos, the mind can take a drama and replay it through all the possible negative outcomes. The label for such an event is worry. It can become a form of self-abuse should you not remedy it by staying conscious and deliberately questioning the rationality of such thoughts or imagined outcomes. The projection of your thoughts should be monitored carefully. The clarity gained by being alert and mindful in anxious moments can help terminate dwelling on past negative outcomes and to centre yourself in the present. It helps to remind yourself that the past is gone and the future does not necessarily replicate the past. A constant state of anxiety can cripple the ability to create the positive future that you would rather have and this should be avoided by taking charge of your thoughts. Your thoughts are your strongest tools in the present moment, and they can be directed to help you dwell on more positive probabilities for the future. Try to anchor yourself as much as possible in the present moment. Being mindful simply means focussing and participating in living the present moment without distraction. Living and taking decisions from this vantage will make you more effective and of a sound mental health. Mind-sets and emotions are the great contributors to your mental health, and you must manage these for your own peace of mind.

Challenging Your Negative Thinking

Thinking is wonderful. Our ability to think means that we can plan, prepare, imagine and fantasise. But thinking can cause us problems too – we can worry, compare, and catastrophise. Many people feel overwhelmed by their thoughts, and problems including anxiety, depression, low self-esteem, paranoia, and pain all have a lot to do with the way we think. Thinking can literally make us sick. In his book 'Why zebras don't get ulcers' the biologist Robert Sapolsky says

A large body of evidence suggests that stress-related diseases emerge, pre- dominantly, out of the fact that we so often activate a physiological system that has evolved for responding to acute physical emergencies, but we turn it on for months on end, worrying about mortgages, relationships, and promotions. What you think and do affects the way you feel and it is not events that bother us, instead it is the way that we interpret them (the thoughts that we have about them).

Thoughts are not facts

Not all of the thinking that happens in our heads is slow, careful, deliberate, or accurate. In his book 'Thinking, Fast and Slow' Daniel Kahneman describes experiments that show the 'short cuts' our brains often prefer to take. When faced with a problem we can choose to respond carefully by thinking of possible solutions and then examining the advantages and disadvantages of each, or we might just have a quick and automatic hunch about how to solve it. It turns out that our brains are surprisingly lazy and bias often creeps into our thinking. We all have quick and automatic thoughts that just 'pop' into our minds. These automatic thoughts are often based on assumptions. Automatic thoughts are often very believable, but they can be inaccurate because they are often not facts.

Depression

Tobi, my friend's 8-year-old daughter, flopped beside me on the sofa, grunting, "I am so depressed you can't believe it. I am missing my friend's party this weekend because we leave on vacation on Friday. To think I already picked out my dress before Mummy confirmed our date of departure".

I could not help laughing out loud but caught myself in time when I saw how important this calamity was to Tobi. I made some sympathetic noises, but it got me thinking about the 'black dog' called depression. Being unhappy isn't the same as being depressed. Depression is a word often used too loosely to describe how we feel after a difficult week at work or when someone gets dumped, but there are specific symptoms and signs to determine whether its depression or just a case of self pity and general annoyance at life. Depression is caused by a chemical imbalance in the body and does not require an annoying or sad event to manifest, although such negative events can trigger or precipitate its manifestation.

The onset of depression is experienced as a changed feeling about life in general. Having a hopeless or helpless outlook on life is the most commonly associated symptom of depression but other feelings include worthlessness, self-hatred, or inappropriate guilt and constant thoughts of *what's the point?*, which is a precursor for suicidal tendencies. A loss of interest in activities that were enjoyed, fatigue, and excessive sleeping should be watched as depression often comes with a lack of energy and an overwhelming feeling of lethargy. Anxiety and irritability are also signs depending on whether you internalize or externalize your feelings. Appetite and weight can fluctuate differently for each person when depressed, while some might comfort-eat, others lose appetite and weight.

The deadly and scariest reality of depression is its connection with suicide. Uncontrollable emotions often lead people to the permanent solution of suicide for what they consider hopeless. Suicides, however, rarely occur without an earlier cry for help; often, prone people would have talked about it with trusted close associates. Family and friends usually recall such cries for help albeit after an avoidable tragedy. Depression affects millions of people; some diagnosed, many not, and most not getting the needed help. Recognizing the symptoms of depression is pivotal to getting or finding the right help. There are varying treatments ranging from lifestyle changes to medications. Exercise and diet are non-medicinal interventions but professional help is required to ensure proper diagnosis and prescription of corrective measures.

Anger—Handling It and Letting Go

We are generally socialized from early in life not to express anger, so emotion is usually repressed in many people. When anger is allowed to build up unmanaged, it can have unhealthy repercussions like lethargy, rage or isolation in extreme cases. Try to see anger as a helpful emotion, as nature's way of flagging what is right and what is not by your reckoning, a guiding force for resolution rather than a source of strife if properly handled. The only solution to dispel this harmful emotion is self-expression, and by this I do not mean fist fights with those who make you angry! Having a chat with the annoying party if possible can usually defuse the situation even if a mild raising of voices becomes inevitable. Where civil communication has however broken down, it might be better if a neutral person, who is able to have a reconciling or calming effect, is involved. Most importantly, once handled, you should let go of the destructive emotion of anger for your own good and sound mind.

Finally, our good or bad health is contributed to and affected by both our physical bodies and our minds. The extent to which we take care of both ultimately decide how well and happy we are.

Chapter 12 - Spirituality

'And I said to the man who stood at the gate of the year:Give me a light that I may tread safely into the unknown.And he replied, Go out into the darkness and put your hand into the Hand of God.That shall be to you better than light and safer than a known way.'

—Minnie Louise Haskins, *"The Gate of the Year"*

We All Have the Quest For a Connection That Guides

The popular name by which this poem is known is "The Gate of the Year"; the author, however, originally named it "God Knows". I have the excerpt from the poem above framed on my desk and have titled it "In the Hands of God". Those of us that this poem resonates with are in very auspicious company as legend has it that the Queen Victoria of the United Kingdom read the poem to the nation on the eve of going into the Second World War. The poem confirms the natural quest or search of every heart for some answers and direction beyond human knowing. I believe that is what spirituality is all about, that need to forge a connection with the divine for the direction we each need.

I am Christian by faith, I belong to a church congregation, and pray fervently. I was, however, born and raised a Muslim. As a youngster I attended an Anglican secondary school where participation in Christian worship was not optional so I went to church during term but prayed five times a day and took the Ramadan fasting seriously according to Islamic tenets when at home. I have also recently come to appreciate the balancing values of meditation, mindfulness, and philosophy. Do I run the risk of being confused because of all of these spiritual influences? I do not believe so.

Spirituality and Religion

'You do not need to work to become spiritual, you are spiritual. You need only to remember that fact. Spirit is within you.'

—Julia Cameron

It is difficult to find a single, widely agreed definition of spirituality. Definitions are broad in range with very limited similarities just because what is termed spiritual can be quite diverse. All in all, spirituality is how we aim to form in the mind, the image of God or the divine. This formation is usually oriented at a mould, which represents the original; Christ in Christianity, Muhammad in Islam, and in Judaism the Torah. We manifest our faith through these different religions to satisfy that human spiritual need for divine connection. Faith is based on the conviction that God exists. It is the acceptance and readiness to be led by the divine will which is practiced through the religions and a person of faith hinges spirituality through religion and religious practices.

Cultural historian William Irwin Thompson puts it succinctly: "Religion is not identical with spirituality; rather religion is the form spirituality takes in manifesting".

Spiritual Practices: Prayer, Mindfulness, and Meditation

Spiritual practices, including meditation, prayer and contemplation, are intended to develop the inner self and lead to an awareness of connectedness with the divine realm. Mindfulness and meditation are devices of stilling the mind from its travels into the past and future to bring you to the reality of the present moment. They help you pay attention to your experiences, thoughts, and emotions to optimise how you participate in life generally. Prayer is all of that and then supplication.

How to Pray? What to Pray?

'How to pray? This is a simple matter. I would say: pray any way you like, so long as you pray.'

—Pope John Paul II

Going by the quote above of one whose life business entails prayers, praying does not come that easily to many. Most of us know we have need of praying but constantly wonder if we do it right; worse still, we dry up when circumstances of life have us bewildered and are desperate for help and answers.

His words should provide some consolation and help in those times of distraction, discouragement, or dryness in your prayer life. The quote has especially made it easier for me to put myself in the presence of God and admit my feeling of inadequacy and just talk! However we pray, I believe God is always near and willing to hear us, help us and answer us. His answer could be a yes, a no, or a wait awhile; whichever one of these it is, you can rest assured in the fact that it is best for you. However, do pray.

Guarding the Door of Your Heart

Like all else in life, your consciousness and active participation in your own spiritual inspiration and growth would protect and direct your heart and life. The spirit man is never totally blank as nature abhors a vacuum; in the absence of wholesome spiritual engagement and faith, there is an emptiness that other things would seek to fill. We ultimately sell out to some belief system, even if it is the cult of friendship or worship at the shrine of intellect or career. Part of a conscious life is being mindful of your spirituality and what may seek to fill that void. Guard the door of your heart and life by remaining spiritually engaged and alert. Personally, as a Christian, I have confidence, hope and rest in the faith that:

The will of God is the measure of all things. The love of God is pure and is poured out through us; His grace is all pervading and inestimable while His mercies are endless. There is nothing small or apparently insignificant that has not been permitted by God – down to the fall of a leaf. God is sufficiently wise, good, powerful, and merciful to turn those events which are apparently the most calamitous to the good if we accept with humility all that His divine will permits.

The Rewards of Spirituality: Grace, Grounding, and Joy

Spirituality provides direction for emotions, values, and a form of footing or assurance in life's journey. For some, being spiritual means going to church, temple, or mosque and participating in religious tenets while for others, it is directed more inwardly and is about the individual finding a quiet place to meditate and reflect about life. Whatever is embraced, manifesting spirituality should make you more likely to be filled with peace, joy, and other positive emotions resulting in positive physiological responses in your life. Spirituality enables us to discover the essence and basis for values by which we want to live, and there would be no purpose whatsoever to a spiritual leaning if it does not affect our actions and attitudes or does not differentiate us in everyday living. Your engagement with society and reactions should be schooled and tempered by your spirituality as your sense of self and mind are expected to be compassionate and more purposeful as a result of your spiritual belief and faith. There are some good fruits of spiritual engagement, and the following especially are profitable.

Contentment and Detachment

'Whatever the good God has given me has always pleased me, even the gifts which have appeared to me less good and less beautiful than those received by others.'

—St Therese of Lisieux

Such acceptance and contentment can be a difficult needle to thread. We live in a world that feeds our desire for more and more until we find it almost impossible to be content with anything ... wealth, position and power, even what we look like! It is natural that we can sometimes get discouraged, jealous, and lacking peace when we see what others have that we think we deserve more, but contentment and detachment can be gained from spirituality. Peace is restored if you learn to shift focus to your blessings and are filled with gratitude for that which has been given to you already. The remedy for a heart that wants endlessly cannot be found in the pursuits of life, only in the self-saving detachment that can be found in spirituality.

'In detachment, the spirit finds quiet and repose for coveting nothing. Nothing wearies it by elation, and nothing oppresses it by dejection, because it stands in the centre of its own humility.'

—St John of the Cross

Surely, such detachment from any external idea or measure of elation or dejection is true liberation.

A Gratitude Mind-Set

The place of grace that spirituality can bring you to with the accompanying manifestation of gratitude is a reward in itself. Gratitude is not merely the appreciation of things because one has come from a place of lack to having, it is rather a state of being, a mind-set; being grateful for just being and for simple everyday things such as a peaceful moment or family.

Does this signify easy contentment and therefore suppression of ambition and endeavour? Far from it! You can be grateful at every stage of life while remaining healthily ambitious and dreaming big. Does a grateful mind-set mean you are in denial of challenges that you grapple with? Again not! Both can work together side by side promoting a peaceful sense of well-being. The more robust your sense of well-being, the stronger it serves as the backdrop to your endeavour, handling challenges, and making the very best of your potential, talents, and opportunities.

Gratitude is more than counting your blessings and feeling fortunate;, it is beyond a mood and can change our relationship with life from that of defence or rejection to that of acceptance and appreciation. A gratitude mind-set turns what we have to enough and in this state of acceptance and feeling grateful; our emotional state and reality are healed.

Your inter-human relationships also benefit immensely from a gratitude mind-set. When you express gratitude to another person, there is an immediate enrichment of the relationship and a surge of happiness, old grievances tend to be erased, and resentments and differences are soothed. There is much to gain by projecting a gratitude mind-set.

Remain Spiritual for Connectedness

Spirituality and being religious are descriptions often considered to be interchangeable. While many religions consider spirituality to be an integral part of their doctrines and practices, there are overlaps between the two. There are also distinct differences between them as well. Because of the exclusivity of some religious teachings, religion tends to separate us from one another, whereas spirituality tends to bring us closer together. Ultimately, it is important that we realize the potential of being connected and learning from everyone despite how different our backgrounds may appear. Life can only be enriched thereby.

Chapter 13 - Ageing

'It is not the young man who should be considered fortunate but the old
man who has lived well, because the young man in his prime wanders
much by chance, vacillating in his beliefs, while the old man has docked in
the harbour, having safeguarded his true happiness.'

—Epicurus

While Epicurus would want the ageing amongst us to feel fortunate, it
takes much courage to feel so as you notice yourself begin to show the
inevitable signs of ageing, sometimes not recognising parts of your
anatomy as the same ones from back then! You would definitely have
safeguarded true happiness though if you are able to approach it with
some humour. How else can you remain unfazed when faced with the
undeniable evidence of an ageing body?

If you are reading this chapter, you are likely to have progressed ap-
preciably on the path of life; and if not, you are a very curious and
forward-planning person. With the ageing territory comes the inevitable softening of body, increasingly grey hair sprouting from more
places than you imagined, a bulging middle despite diet efforts, failing
short-term memory with a tendency to repeat old stories, wrinkling
face, neck and hands for all to see - the list is endless! Rather than be-
moaning these signs, it is helpful to consider the fact that those who
experience old age are definitely fortunate not to have died young.
That thought should help you become mindful to enjoy this segment
of your journey; after all, you will only get older. You might one day,

when you attain very old age, look back to now and long for the good old days!

Aging Gracefully

In his search for what he calls 'authentic old age', how aging should be like, Daniel Klein, in his book *Travels with Epicurus*, draws attention to the pleasures that are available only later in life. His quest started from his concerns about what he considers to be the modern day worship at the temple of youth, the great effort that we all are expending to avert the acknowledgement of old age ... and the war chest for the battle is getting bigger and richer with extreme and extremely expensive procedures to de-age. He wonders if by being preoccupied with all such, we might actually be missing out on a valuable stage of life in fighting it or trying to wish it away.

Bravely, Klein declared himself an old man at 73 and sought the most satisfying way to live this stage from the example of the contentedly old on the Greek Island of Hydra.

I personally own up to vanity and refuse to accept the creed that says the body should be left to its own devises, untended, just because one has attained a certain age. I however hear his warning. The 'forever young' trap can be exhausting and the 'trying too hard' look is not so attractive if not downright hilarious sometimes! Tight clothes, too much makeup on maturing ladies, or a bright yellow Ferrari and cut-out sleeves on maturing men can all signify panic at impending old age.

Klein's concern is that in trying to stretch out the prime of life indefinitely, and denying old age for as long as possible, many miss out on a slower yet pleasantly fulfilling stage of life. He believes they could end up spinning from forever prime straight into what he termed old oldage, where senility and age-related illness reside and then soon, death. This sounds to me like not giving oneself an opportunity to slow down gracefully. Scary thought that, jogging with rippling muscles in tight lycra one day and totally out of it the next! What he advocates is finding that place of authentically and contentedly aging. This would allow aging people be rational and honest with themselves about the likely time left for them and how to use it in the best and most satisfying way that is not a constant struggle and insistence not to be considered old. Vanity makes me believe he is not suggesting the aging should   necessarily forget to remain fashionably well-dressed and groomed as appropriate for their age.

Old Age Can Spring a Surprise!

One minute you're on the school run, manoeuvring a fast-moving career while also keeping an eye on fashion, the next you're pondering the strange allure of clothes that hang loosely. It happens almost overnight and feels like being thrown over some invisible wall into middle age, where there are no guidelines or maps to help you navigate the confusing territory.

I was 59 when I wrote the original edition of this book. When my grandmother was 59, I considered her an old woman. When my mother was 59, she was a grandmother and an ageing adult in ways that I still don't feel or would before I turn 70.. The surprise is not just about looks and fashion, it is the whole works; relationships, family, children, work; how technology moves so bafflingly fast, and you are increasingly not classified as youth - your age classification on forms become 50 to 65! Really? You are still in your fifties and being classified with 65-year-olds? How does one navigate these confusing and potentially treacherous waters? Can Botox and similar fixes be your friend, or are they just plain dangerous? I often wondered why there is the phenomenon of middle-age crisis for which there is never a clear definition of what it entails. Now, it is old-age crisis that I look out for. Middle age or old age, there need not be a crisis or an unpleasant surprise if we consciously transit from one stage of life to another, happy to embrace each new stage with grace and some curiosity.

'Getting old is like climbing a mountain, you get a little breathless, but the view is much better.'

—Ingrid Bergman

When I read a blog by Ari Cohen sometime ago, I became much more emboldened and hopeful in looking forward to the senior tranche of life. It made me want to better take care of myself and not be fearful. She had put into words my own hopes for growing further up, a real encouragement for graceful aging without fear.

She apparently had an affinity for older people because of a close relationship with her grandmother, who she admired for her sense of style and considered much more fun than her teenage mates. She had moved to New York and noticed a dearth of representation of aging people in the media in an attractive or vibrant way. She saw a disproportionate focus on youthfulness and what little she found about older women was mostly about failing health and the fear of aging. She then started her project, aptly tagged Advanced Style, photographing and blogging about vibrant and stylish seniors living vital and joyful lives on their own terms. Her blog shows it is possible.

Refreshing Life through Later Generations

The idea of a generational influence is usually viewed from the passing of legacy and history from an older generation to a later one. The impact and influence of the ensuing generations on life as we age is however worth thinking about before the eventide of life arrives. This is useful for two reasons. The first is the joy and refreshment that actively participating in the life of your children, their children and other young people can bring to your aging self. The second is the learning opportunities that both generations can provide each other and immensely gain from.

I have been particularly fortunate in the impact that my children's lives, education, and experiences have and continue to have on the evolvement of my own life. As each of my two sons, with their eight-year age gap, have grown from babies to young children, students in schools and universities into young adults in careers, I have been privileged to participate in their lives, making acquaintances and some firm friends along the way. I feel that I have lived many lives in many layers through my children and hope to experience more with their children. I have met the most interesting people from diverse cultures through them, thereby acquiring tastes and lifestyles later in life just because I am the mother of the boys. Those experiences also make it easy for me to relate exceptionally with other young people and exchange refreshing ideas with them.

Your opportunity to enjoy and be impacted by the activities of later generations will be dictated by how available you are and how consciously you are willing to participate. Aging need not be boring or regretful; it is a stage that can be refreshed by children, grandchildren, and non-family contacts of ensuing generations.

Great Freedom Comes with Aging

'Old age has a great sense of calm and freedom.'

—Plato

Nothing prepared me for the mental freedom that arrived with my 50th birthday. I was really never afraid of getting older, probably because I was always too busy to ponder the matter, or because I have always had much older friends who I adore and who motivate me. None of my older friends had bemoaned their age or acted in ways that show regret at their increasing chronological numbers. The only thought my security conscious self ever gave to aging was building of structures, systems, and affordability for a time when I would no longer be in a salaried career and my work-related society and structures would need to be replaced. I had looked forward to doing things I had not been able to do in my prime due to the obligations of work, family, and children when maturity arrived. I hope plan for an active old age. I envision it without developing any misgivings, fears, or anxieties of its onset.

I consider my fifties the most liberating and confident phase of my life so far. Work has new meaning, the urgency that attends work now emanates from the fulfilment from creating value in whatever I do. My consideration for work has shifted from myself to others, and that has brought an amazing emotional reward.

Self-knowledge, mastery of one's emotions, and an acceptance of how life has played out over the decades would help make aging pleasant and peaceful. This stage of life should not be blighted by regrets leading to depression and other neurotic afflictions. A thoughtful person, as age progresses, will see clearly the patterns that have defined his or her past and know to accept what cannot be changed and change what can be salvaged. Fifty was the magic age for me as regards accepting and being grateful for what and who I had become; it was finally time for dropping off the baggage of wishes that were obviously not 'given' to me to be or have. This acceptance of reality freed me to use my life experiences so far to build a fulfilling line of work while gaining the freedom to participate effectively through different stages of my children's development. I could not have wanted better than that outcome.

Fortunately, in many cultures, the ageing and the aged command deep respect because time tested wisdom is known to reside with them. I personally do not see the old amongst us as worn and obsolete, to be dumped in a corner, ignored, or at best barely tolerated. I see them as vessels of treasure; history, experience, and useful advice that we would be wise to tap into.

While technology makes the new world very advanced and easier in some ways, the fundamentals don't change from generation to generation. There is nothing new under the sun as the wise and rich King Solomon declared way back in biblical days and he has yet to be proven wrong. Nothing new about family dynamics, ambition, achievements, the desires of humans, the demons that plague, life cycles, love, contention for power, cycles of abundance, and crashes – the list is endless. They remain the issues we grapple with, and they were discussed in his songs and proverbs with such insight that make Solomon's submissions still applicable today. The insights from elders provide very useful perspective if only we pay attention to them.

Some Advice for Enjoyable Old Age.

- Some people embrace their golden years, while others become bitter and surly. Life is too short to waste your days on the latter. Spend your time with positive, cheerful people, it'll rub off on you and your days will seem that much better. Spending your time with bitter people will make you older and harder to be around.

- Be proud, both inside and out. Keep grooming. When you are well-maintained on the outside, it seeps in, making you feel proud and strong.

- Always stay up to date. Read newspapers, watch the news. Go online and read what people are saying. Make sure you have an active email account and try to use some of those social networks. Keeping in touch with what is going on and with the people you know is important at any age.

- Never use the phrase: "In my time." Your time is now. As long as you're alive, you are part of this time. You may have been younger, but you are still you now, having fun and enjoying life.

- Don't abandon your hobbies. If you don't have any, take up new ones. You can travel, hike, cook, read, dance. You can adopt a cat or a dog, grow a garden, play cards, chess, or golf. You can paint, volunteer or just collect certain items. Find something you like and spend some real time having fun with it.

- Some pain and discomfort can come with getting older. Try not to dwell on them but accept them as a part of the cycle of life. Get medical help and try to minimize them in your mind. They are not who you are, they are something that life added to you. If they become your entire focus, you lose sight of the person you used to be.

- Laugh. Laugh A LOT. Laugh at everything. Remember, you are one of the lucky ones. You managed to have a life, a long one. Many never get to this age, never get to experience a full life. But you did. So, what's not to laugh about? Find the humour and gratitude in your situation.

Afterword

Now that LIFE has been considered in its different aspects and seasons, we all know that some of those slices happen concurrently such that each slice or aspect influence the others and are affected by them in return. In order to hold it all together while dealing with the different aspects simultaneously, it is a constant and effortless consciousness that you need to develop such that every day, every event, every thought, every action is permeated by primordial attention and your well settled intentions.

Living life carelessly and recklessly can happen easily if you do not have a script for your life to which you are committed and deliberately follow. To avoid constant distraction from your script, it is important that you build a supporting and protective ecosystem for the life and lifestyle you desire; you need to mind who, and what constitute your constant environment; the friends, counsel and physical setting you are exposed to. Are they nourishing and promoting or do they pose risks to your life plans. Your ecosystem, and daily actions should help you preserve your journey's direction and not undermine the expedition that is your life.

By becoming and remaining conscious, mindful, and intentional in the different aspects of life, you can format your desired lifestyle and achieve your own balance that will fulfil and satisfy you. The point of a conscious life is to achieve a satisfying balance from the convergence of all areas and aspects of life that is gratifying and joyful; to make you able to consider your life and be constantly proud and grateful.

The quote that says "The best way to predict the future is to create it" is too true! I implore you to create the future you prefer. I hope the preceding chapters have answered for you the question *how*? For each of us, our present circumstances are the sum total of our beliefs and actions of the past; for better or worse, we have built the life we have today. Outside influences play some role, but for the most part, how we use our time, invest, or spend our money and what we focus on inevitably have mostly created the life we have. Rarely does any one action or decision have a huge impact, but the cumulative effect is undeniable. Day by day, action by action, choice by choice we create our own lives.

Many people claim to be too busy, too stressed, or struggling to survive that no time or attention is invested to create the future. Happenstance is another excuse usually proffered. True, we cannot underestimate the nature and effect of happenstance when considering a person's fate; how being in a particular place at a particular time can change the entire course of things making you seem like a hostage to life's random happenings. The truth remains that within all of that, we each remain responsible for our responses, choices, and actions. Your consciousness or lack of it does affect how much and for how long happenstance can affect or derail your journey. Those who ride the tides of life better have 'unusual awareness' – otherwise known as consciousness of themselves and their intentions. Their consciousness make them more adaptable to changes or happenstance; they are very quick to perceive anything that might threaten or indeed facilitate their plans. Successful people are awake thinking, planning, and taking actions so happenstance rarely defeat them.

Finally, there are those who sleepwalk through life. They often work hard and hope for some breakthrough, but not having written the script of their own life, they live according to the script life throws them.

Hopefully, that is not you!

Sources

Outliers: Malcolm Gladwell (United Kingdom. Little Brown and Company 2008)

Committed: Elizabeth Gilbert (United States. Viking Press 2010)

Surprised by Joy: C. S. Lewis (United Kingdom. Geoffrey Bles 1955)

Stillness Speaks: Eckhart Tolle (United States. New World Library 2003)

Those Bloomin Kids: Joy Haney (United States. Radiant Life Publications 1994)

Build Your Family Bank: Emily Griffiths-Hamilton (Canada. Figuire1 Publishing 2014)

Strong Father, Strong Daughter: Meg Meeker (United States. Ballantine Books 2007)

The Monk who Sold his Ferrari: Robin Sharma (United States. Harper Collins 1997)

Travels with Epicurus: Daniel Klein (United Kingdom. Penguin Publishing Group 2014)

The Faith of Barack Obama: Stephen Mansfield (United States. Thomas Nelson 2011)

Why Zebras Don't Get Ulcers: Robert Sapolsky (United States. W. H. Freeman (2nd ed.), Holt Paperbacks (3rd ed.))

Thinking Fast and Slow: Daniel Kahneman (United States. Farrar, Straus and Giroux)

Index

D

E

M

N

Y

ABOUT THE AUTHOR

Funmi Oyetunji is a Chartered Accountant and a Fellow of the Certified and Chartered Accountants Association in the UK. Her career has spanned over forty years covering accounting practice and consulting in the UK; Banking as the corporate treasurer of the largest bank in Nigeria; and now Investment Portfolio Management.

Funmi has put her life experiences and counseling skills into mentoring as a life and business coach. She has also taught finance on the executive programs at the Lagos Business School and is frequently invited for speaking engagements.

Funmi Oyetunji has served and still serves as a non-executive independent director on the boards of a number of quoted companies. She chairs the LASAL Foundation, a charity dedicated to social mobility through academic scholarships.

ABOUT THE BOOK

A Conscious Life is a detailed and practical book about life in which the author covers the different stages and aspects of life, helping to signpost the critical junctions and timelines that the reader can expect to navigate on the journey of life.

The Author proposes a life where a person takes charge and responsibility for his or her life to live in an intentional and focused manner that would conduce to a fulfilling life by their own measure.

The book provides a practical guide for different stages and aspects of life which is arranged such that it does not have to be read in sequence. Each reader can dip into the relevant chapters or sections depending on their particular life stage, situation or need for counsel at different times. This makes A Conscious Life a veritable reference book for all seasons of life.